100 YEARS AND STILL COUNTING

THE TOWN OF CASS, WV

by Gerald M. Futej & Max S. Robin

ACKNOWLEDGMENTS

John P. Killoran at Oats Run on the Cass Scenic Railroad, May 17, 1975. (Photo by Gerald M. Futej)

There are very few times that we meet someone that has the foresight to see an opportunity and the ability to make that opportunity a reality. While the spark for saving the railroad at Cass is generally attributed to Russell Baum, the Company Town of Cass was saved in large part by the efforts of John P. Killoran. As Assistant Director of State Parks for the West Virginia Department of Natural Resources, John inherited responsibility for the railroad at the State Park at Cass.

As a historian and rail buff he was a loving custodian of the State's first railroad. In his words "It's a short railroad but just as wide as any other!" But John saw beyond the railroad. He embraced the local logging history; the saw mill, the Company Store and the Company houses in town. He and his wife, Nancy, bought part ownership in one of the small frame houses in East Cass, complete with hand pump for water on the front porch. It was always open for one more visitor.

I had less than 10 visits with John before he moved his family to Alaska. They were almost always at Railfan Weekend at Cass, and he always greeted my family and me with open arms. John was eulogized in 2005 as having "an infectious smile". There is no better way to describe him. Almost always with a pipe clenched in his teeth, he would shepherd the railfan photo line with a bull horn. Stopping to remind you individually, if necessary, of the need for safety, but always with a smile.

It's hard to imagine any one else could convince the State to buy a bunch of seventy-year-old houses in a town next to a closed saw mill. John did it. He had help, to be sure, but without his vision and involvement we would not have Cass to visit today. Thank you, John. Please keep looking out for Cass.

We thank John Killoran and the State of West Virginia for saving the structures at Cass for us. We also thank those that worked individually to preserve the history of Cass in text and photos. This work is based largely on the published works of Roy B. Clarkson and Harry Dunkin, both natives of Cass, and we thank them for their insight. Just as important are the photos taken by the late Phil Bagdon and Ivan O. Clarkson, as well as Sonny Burruss and George Fizer that are presented here. Research by William P. McNeel at the courthouse in Marlinton has filled the gaps regarding ownership of the land. Discussions with current and former residents of Cass have given us a better understanding of growing up and living in a Company Town.

The current and former members of the staff of the Cass Scenic Railroad State Park have been most supportive of our efforts. Similarly the staffs at the Pocahontas County Historical Society, the West Virginia State Archives, and the West Virginia University Library were key to finding many of the vintage photos included here. We thank them all collectively for their help.

A special thanks to my daughter Katie for her masterful use of desktop publishing as well as making us meet deadlines. The patience of our wives, Barbara and Kathe, is greatly appreciated.

Thank you all, without your help this would not be possible.

Gerald M. Futej
Max S. Robin

Privately Funded & Published by
Greenhill Station Productions
1376 Green Hill Avenue
West Chester, PA 19380

Gerald M. Futej - Owner, Editor
Max S. Robin - Historical Editor

Table of Contents

The Town of Cass ... by Max S. Robin   Page 4

The Company Store at Cass ... by Roy B. Clarkson

                 & Gerald M. Futej   Page 34

Sunday Services ... by Gerald M. Futej   Page 50

School Days ... by Max S. Robin & Gerald M. Futej   Page 52

Neither Snow, Nor Rain ... by Gerald M. Futej   Page 62

I Remember Cass ... compiled by Gerald M. Futej   Page 64

A Cass Connection ... by Gerald M. Futej   Page 72

The Houses at Cass... by Max S. Robin   Page 80

Restoring a House at Cass .... by John Glaab   Page 96

Doctor's House in HO Scale .... by John Glaab   Page 100

Front St., Cass, W. Va.

907

An early postcard, ca 1905, showing the Company houses on Front Street at Cass. Note the wire mesh fences, the wooden boardwalk, and the unique porch railings on the original houses. Seven of the nine houses shown are still in existence and all but one of those are still in use. (Photographer unknown, collection of Pocahontas County Historical Society)

The Town of Cass
by Max S. Robin

Background

Cass, West Virginia represents a unique example of what was once considered a common American community – the Company Town. These towns were built by companies, often family owned, to provide housing and a shopping facility for the employees. Probably the most common, and long-lived, towns of this type were developed to facilitate coal mining, precious metal mining, and timber harvesting, along with the production of valuable wood products. Construction of these towns was generally to meet the immediate Company requirements, rather than longevity. Generally the natural resources at a single location were expended in ten to twenty years and company housing only needed to last that long. Cass was certainly unique in that respect, all of the

buildings constructed displayed the expectation of their existence and use for an indefinite period. The use of thick hardwood floors, for example, supported that expectation. The inclusion of the town of Cass in the Cass Scenic Railroad State Park and its listing on the National Register of Historic Places confirm its unique character and background during more than a century of existence.

After the Civil War, and extending through the beginning of the 20th century, the United States experienced a new reason for westward and southward expansion. It was not related to the individual desire to own a piece of land as a place to live and support a family. It was the continuing exploration for new deposits of natural resources such as coal and wood. Those staple resources were required to support the

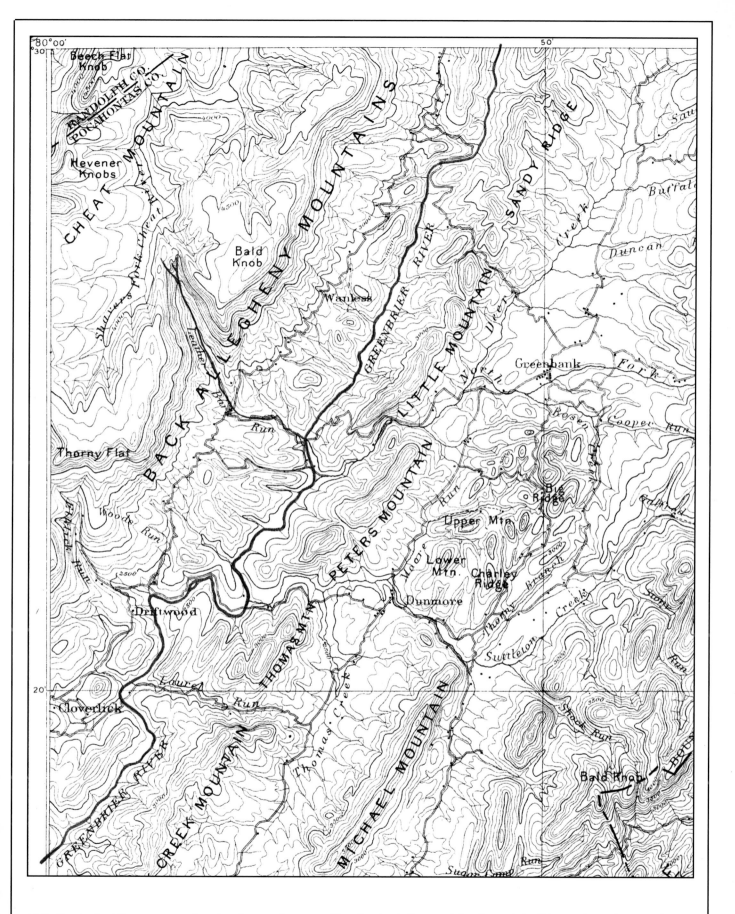

U.S. Geological Survey map showing the confluence of Leatherbark Run and the Greenbrier River, where the road from Greenbank crossed at the ford, as surveyed in 1887. (U.S. Department of the Interior, collection of Gerald M. Futej)

Undated portrait of the family that changed Pocahontas County and the entire papermaking industry; (front row l to r) John G. Luke, Rose Luke (mother), William Luke (father), David L. Luke, (back row l to r) William A. Luke, Thomas Luke, James Luke, Isabelle Luke and Adam Luke. (Photographer unknown, courtesy Cass Scenic Railroad State Park)

unprecedented growth and the industrial revolution that the country was experiencing. Many firms which provided these two commodities were finding they were reaching the limits of availability of these resources in the northeastern states, such as New York and Pennsylvania. Reports of large, seemingly endless, forests with numerous species of both hardwood and softwood trees, coupled with equally bountiful mineral resources led to the serious consideration of the development of West Virginia by many of the natural resource producing companies of the Northeastern states.

The Luke Family

William Luke was a trained and experienced second generation Scottish papermaker. He migrated to the United States in 1852 and established a successful paper mill in Manayunk, near Philadelphia,

Pennsylvania. His success as a papermaker planted the seed for the events that ultimately led to the construction of what was to become the town of Cass in Pocahontas County, West Virginia. Three of William's sons, John G., William A., and David L., eventually followed in his footsteps and became deeply involved in the manufacturing of paper and all of its ancillary processes. Early in their papermaking careers the Luke brothers realized there were two overwhelming issues which had huge impacts on the product quality and profitability of all paper manufacturing facilities. They determined that every paper mill required consistent quality pulp which, in turn, depended upon a continuous supply of pulpwood.

The availability of consistent, high quality pulp for use in the papermaking process determined the quality of the paper. The Lukes believed that the then-new, and commercially unproven, chemical "sulphite" process of preparing pulp was the key to the future of mass producing high quality paper. The sulphite process made use of calcium sulphite, in conjunction with lead-lined processing vessels, to separate the wood pulp from the lignum which binds the wood fibers to each other. John convinced his father, William, to finance the technical education of his younger brother David, who later graduated from the University of Pennsylvania with degrees in both Chemistry and Chemical Engineering.

The Lukes formed the Piedmont Pulp and Paper Company in Alleghany County, Maryland. Construction of a pulp mill started in May 1889 and was completed prior to year's end. The older brothers' papermaking experience and manufacturing expertise, coupled with David's advanced knowledge of chemistry, enabled them to establish the first commercially successful chemical manufacturing process for pulping wood. By 1891 they formed a second firm, West Virginia Paper Company. The Lukes designed and managed the construction of a new papermaking facility, which was producing quality paper by January 1892.

The success of both facilities was dependent upon the guarantee of an abundant supply of continuously available pulpwood. Regardless of weather conditions, seasons of the year, or the relative locations of the timber reserves and the papermill, the supply of pulpwood was essential. In 1892 the Luke family purchased 50,000 acres of virgin spruce forest in Tucker County, West Virginia, near the town of Davis. This ensured a sufficient supply of high quality pulpwood for the first paper mill built and controlled by West Virginia Paper Company. This primal forest provided an unprecedented 30,000 to 50,000 board feet of wood per acre. By 1895, the Luke's third company, the West Virginia Pulp Company, was in full production at Davis, West Virginia. It produced over 30,000 pounds of pulp per day. The combined output of the Luke's two pulp mills produced enough high grade pulp to enable the paper company to ship over 40,000 pounds of paper per day. Considered to be amongst the finest paper anywhere, it was shipped worldwide.

The West Virginia Pulp and Paper Company of West Virginia was formed on November 10, 1897 with the intent of merging all the Luke holdings into one new corporation. This occurred on December 7, 1897, when all the original Luke companies authorized the sale of their properties and assets to the new corporation. As a result, on April 26, 1898, all of the original individual Luke companies were dissolved and West Virginia Pulp and Paper Company emerged. The formation of this new corporate entity in 1898 precipitated three significant events in 1899, which directly led to the creation of the town that was to become Cass, West Virginia.

The Lukes decided to build another, larger, pulp and paper plant complex south of the vast spruce forests of West Virginia. For various environmental reasons and the availability of existing rail transportation, the town of Covington, Virginia was chosen as the location for the new manufacturing facility.

Forest surveys showed that spruce trees did not grow east of the small town of Green Bank, West Virginia, near the Greenbrier River. However, the spruce forests were essentially continuous in the high mountains to the west, bounded by the Gauley and the Greenbrier Rivers. A large portion of Pocahontas County was drained by the Greenbrier River and Shavers Fork of Cheat River. Envisioning continued growth and expansion of their fledgling paper making empire, the Lukes purchased 67,619 contiguous acres of virgin woodlands on Cheat Mountain in 1899. Located astride the border of Randolph and Pocahontas counties of West Virginia, it was classified as "spruce land". The property was purchased from James H. Dewing of Kalamazoo, Michigan. This was but the first purchase of many huge tracts of spruce forest acquired by the new firm along Cheat Mountain in Pocahontas, Randolph, and Davis counties. Ultimately, by 1920 West Virginia Pulp and Paper Company owned or leased approximately 300,000 acres in this area of West Virginia to provide pulpwood.

John Luke was well aware that the reason he was able to purchase the Dewing Tract at a reasonable price was in large part due to the difficulty Mr. Dewing had encountered in trying to float cut timber down the Cheat River to his own saw mill in Point Marion, Pennsylvania. However, the Lukes were also aware of the ongoing construction by the Chesapeake and Ohio Railroad (C&O) of a branch from the East-West main line, which ran from Newport News, Virginia to Cincinnati, Ohio. The new branch ran almost due north from Ronceverte to Durbin, West Virginia; roughly paralleling the Greenbrier River for approximately 92 miles. At a point south of Green Bank, Leatherbark Creek entered the Greenbrier River from the west. This area was variously known as Leatherbark Crossing or Leatherbark Ford. The C&O railroad expected to reach this point in 1902 and the Luke's surveyors had plotted a feasible route for a logging railroad to be built starting at this location and initially heading west, parallel to Leatherbark Creek. It was decided that this was the most appropriate place to construct the logging railroad repair facilities, a saw mill and the infrastructure required for the employees who would support the anticipated pulpwood and timber production.

Concurrent with these actions, the Lukes realized that a source of ready capital was needed to support this rapid and extensive expansion. John Luke had previously very successfully, and profitably, managed the Tyrone, Pennsylvania paper mill of the Morrison, Bare, and Cass Company. He was aware that Mr. Morrison had withdrawn from that firm to operate another mill he owned and that Mr. Bare had passed away in 1890. He was also aware of the cash flow that mill generated for its current owner. The sole remaining owner was Mr. Joseph K. Cass. John Luke approached Mr. Cass about merging their two companies. An agreement was quickly reached and in 1899 The West Virginia Pulp and Paper Company of Delaware (WVP&P Co.) was formed. John Luke and Joseph Cass were both named as directors of the new firm. The merger provided WVP&P Co. the capital it required for expansion. It also provided Joseph Cass a generous rate of return on his investment.

Although the Lukes were in the pulp supply and the papermaking businesses, they realized that the vast timberlands that they controlled would also provide an incredibly rich source of highly desirable and marketable timber. In addition to the spruce which they viewed as their primary source of pulpwood, the forests contained desirable trees of both hardwood and softwood varieties. It was quickly apparent that they were going to need a lumber sales organization. An experienced and respectable lumberman to manage and direct this part of their operations was required. Due to their previous familiarity with the Whitmer Lumber Company at Bayard, West Virginia and the Condon-Lane Boom and Lumber Company at Horton, West Virginia, they were aware of Samuel Slaymaker and his excellent reputation. Mr. Slaymaker and the fledgling WVP&P Co. reached an agreement which proved to be an asset far more valuable than they could possibly have foreseen. Acting upon Mr. Slaymaker's advice, WVP&P Co. hired Emory P. Shaffer as General Superintendent of the pulpwood and lumber operations located at the mouth of Leatherbark Creek. These two men were largely responsible for the successful

Samuel E. Slaymaker of Philadelphia, Pennsylvania, managed the sales and marketing of the product from the saw mill at Cass. (Photographer unknown, West Virginia and Regional History Collection, West Virginia University Libraries)

Emory P. Shaffer, Superintendent of the WVP&P Co. operations at Cass, with his wife, Pattie Hannah Shaffer, and their children on the steps of their residence at Cass. (Photographer unknown, collection of Pocahontas County Historical Society)

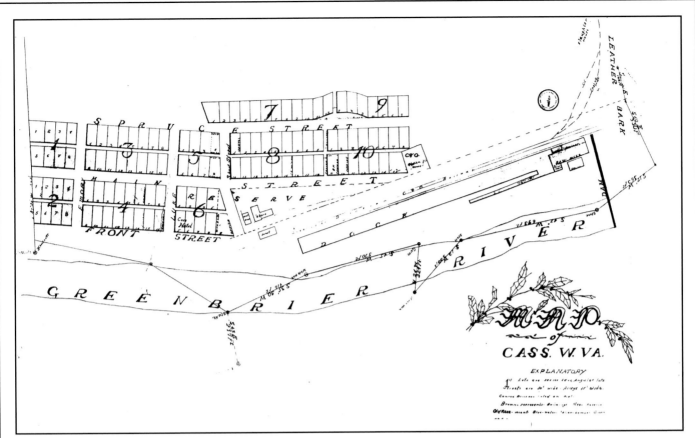

The original plan for development of the WVP&P Co. property at Cass. (Pocahontas County Deed Book, courtesy William P. McNeel)

lumber marketing and sales activities, as well as the daily operations at Cass for over three decades. Their responsibilities included timber harvesting, lumber production, the associated railroad operations that connected them, and the Company Town of Cass itself.

Company Town

The use of the name "Cass" to describe the area encompassing the lumber operations, the saw mill, and the logging railroad maintenance facilities appears to have been first used in a letter from Sam Slaymaker to Emory Shaffer dated August 2, 1900. The name was chosen to honor and give public recognition to Joseph K. Cass, former owner of the Morrison and Cass Paper Co. of Tyrone, Pennsylvania and Vice President of WVP&P Co., a position he would hold for several decades.

The first WVP&P Co. structure built at Cass was a boarding house which stood approximately where the Railroad Depot stands today. This structure, originally built to provide housing for the primarily Italian immigrant railroad construction employees, became the hub of what was officially called Camp One. Early in March 1901, the main residential area of Cass was

formally surveyed by R. H. Boal. Three north-south streets were laid out roughly parallel to the Greenbrier River; named Front Street (overlooking the C&O Greenbrier subdivision tracks), Main Street (now also known as WV Route 66), and Spruce Street (also called High Street or Church Street depending on the particular time frame under discussion). The intersecting east-west streets were Short Street (closest to the Company Store), Luke Street, and Emory Street, which was the southernmost of these streets. All the streets were 50 feet wide. The housing lots predominantly had 50 feet of street frontage and were 100 feet deep from front to back. The north-south streets were additionally separated by 15 foot wide alleys. The alleys were lined with a fuel shed and an outhouse behind each building. The fuel sheds were initially for wood, but were used in later years for coal storage.

All the Company houses built on those lots were equipped with running water and electricity when built. Intended for rental to employees, the Company Houses were provided with water and electricity generated at the saw mill. The utilities were included in the monthly house rent. Subsequent records indicate that the Company installed bathrooms in all of those

Main St., Cass, W. Va.

Looking north on Main Street from a postcard printed by the Pocahontas Supply Company. Under construction, at right, is the two story Odd Fellows Hall. It was built next to the former site of the first school at Cass which was closed in 1908. (Archives Collection, West Virginia State Archives)

This undated photo of Cass, which shows 24 Company Houses, several of which appear to be still under construction, was taken before the construction of the Presbyterian Church or the Masonic Lodge Hall. (A. Norman Smith Collection, West Virginia State Archives)

The Masonic Lodge Hall shows prominent here at the southwest corner of Front Street and Luke Street across from the Baker House Hotel, at the extreme right. South of the Hall is the original Presbyterian Church and 35 Company Houses. The end of the steel bridge at the extreme right corner indicates this photo was taken between 1908 and 1918. (Mrs. James Tucker Collection, West Virginia State Archives)

The end of the concrete bridge at the lower right corner indicates this photo was taken after 1922. It shows 51 Company Houses, the second and the third schools at Cass, and nine of the one story houses at "colored bottom". The Presbyterian Church has been renovated with the offset bell tower and entrance. (Meadow River Lumber Collection, West Virginia State Archives)

houses between 1918 and 1920, thus eliminating the need for the outhouses.

The Company built three distinctly different size and style houses for rent by its employees. The class of house you could rent was based on the relative importance of your job within the Company. Class Three Houses were for day-laborers, Class Two Houses were for section foremen and office personnel, and Class One Houses were for employees in management positions. Virtually all of the Company-owned buildings in Cass were sheathed, or "weatherboarded", with what was known as "German" siding, a narrow beveled-edge horizontal siding introduced in the early 1900's.

The Class Three Houses were built as rectangular two story six room houses with gabled roof. Each was built with shed-roofed front and rear porches. It appears that all were built to a standard floor plan with at least one double hung window in each room. A single chimney rose through the center of the house and allowed for connection of stoves from each room. Early photographs show nine houses along Front Street, nine more along the east side of Main Street, eleven on the west side of Main Street, and five houses on the east side of Spruce Street. As many as 51 Class Two and Class Three Houses can be counted in photos taken in the mid-1920's. Later photos show additional houses along Spruce Street. The exact sequence of construction, however, is unknown.

It appears that the Class Two Houses were developed in later years by adding on to the standard Class Three Houses. Many of these had a two story wing at right angle to the standard house, which resulted in an L-shaped floor plan. Some were built longer front to back or with porches along the side of the house. It seems these were built on larger lots or on corner lots.

The false work used during construction of the concrete bridge over the Greenbrier River is visible in this view from the original Greenbank Road. (Photographer unknown, collection of Pocahontas County Historical Society)

The Class One Houses, for the Company managers, were also built at Company expense. However their designs, details, and sizes were modified at their occupants' requests. Five of these houses were originally built along Back Mountain Road on "Big Bug Hill". Their fronts were on the east side facing the Greenbrier River. The handsome facades of these buildings were seldom seen and the front entrances appear to have been rarely used. These buildings appear to have been based on the standard Class Three House design; the front and stairway side of each having similar window arrangements and roof lines. The houses appear to have been built at least one-third longer, front to back, than the Class Three Houses. The extra space was used for an additional two rooms and entrance hall space. A board walk from Luke Street, built partially on an elevated trestle spanning the drop-off south of the property frontages, was built along the front of these houses and connected to the Company Store property by a series of wooden staircases.

Another Class One House was built at a later date on the corner of Spruce and Luke Streets (#345 facing Luke Street), intended to house the lumber company's Superintendent. The house has a north facing front, complemented by a four bay veranda graced with large Ionic columns and an extremely attractive railing. Unlike any of the other buildings in Cass, this house has a tall outside chimney at the east gable. The dwelling has a somewhat regal appearance, contributed to by its setting high above the street junction.

The last of the Class One Houses was the "Doctor's House'; considered by many Cass residents and visitors over the years to be one of the most architecturally attractive homes in the town. This building sits on the west side of Back Mountain Road on the side of the hill overlooking the Greenbrier River and the bridge to East Cass. It is a large, square, two story structure with halls running the length of the house on both levels. The northeast front is a standard two bay facade. However, it has an off-center entrance

The Doctor's House and his office to the left was used by Dr. Uriah Hannah from 1914 until 1943. Dr. Hannah cared for the local community residents as well as the WVP&P Co. employees and their families. (Ivan O. Clarkson, collection West Virginia State Archives)

The Baker House Hotel at the corner of Front Street and Luke Street was home to many WVP&P Co. employees who lived at Cass without families. (Photographer unknown, collection of Tammy Shoemaker, courtesy Sonny Burruss)

doorway from the columned veranda. The veranda extends across the entire front of the house and halfway across the northern side of the house. Each side of this building has a two story bay projection with three windows at each floor. A small one story Doctor's Office was located just south of the house.

Housing was only one of the necessities provided by the Company. The Pocahontas Supply Company was a subsidiary of WVP&P Co. It provided a convenient source of supplies for living and working at Cass, as well as on the mountain. Residents could purchase food, clothing, tools, and building supplies at the "Company Store". Located close to the C&O railroad station it served the entire community. Company employees and their families were allowed to buy on credit. At the end of a pay period the purchases were deducted from the employee's pay. Meat was provided by the S.B. Nethken & Company Meat Market, located adjacent to the Company Store. Fresh vegetables and livestock were raised on the nearby Company Farm along Deer Creek.

WVP&P Co. also provided other vital community services. It provided space for a U.S. Post office, the Presbyterian church on Front Street, and the Masonic Lodge next to it. The Baker House Hotel between the Masonic Lodge and the Company Store provided housing for employees without families and the transient travelers to the area. The two story hotel was actually comprised of two separate buildings several feet apart and connected by porches which extended across the gap, facing Front Street. Later known as The Mountain Inn, this hotel provided long term residences for mostly mill workers and train crews, who had the $1.00-$1.50 per day room and board charge deducted directly from their Company paycheck. By 1920, the hotel boasted four indoor bathrooms. One of these buildings is still standing and continues to be in use.

A local connection to both national telegraph and telephone service was established and later the Company built its own telephone system connecting Cass, Spruce, and Slaty Fork. This was one of the first private telephone networks built. The switchboard was located on the second floor of the meat market.

The construction of a hospital and hiring of a Company doctor provided local medical services. Dr.

The front of the Company hospital accentuates its distinctive curved porches. Closed early in the 1920's, it served later as a residence for E.P. Shaffer and afterward as a Boarding House. (Photo by Ivan O. Clarkson, collection of Sonny Burruss)

Julien D. Arbuckle became the "town" doctor in 1901. His brother Dr. J.A. Arbuckle practiced as his partner from 1901 through 1903. At that time Dr. Henry Ward Randolph became the resident medical doctor in Cass. The doctor's job encompassed treating not just those who lived or worked in Cass. He also served the loggers and other WVP& P Co. employees working in the woods along the Cheat River, and those residing or working near Durbin, 11 miles north of Cass along the Greenbrier River.

Dr. Uriah Hevener Hannah was hired in 1907 by West Virginia Spruce Lumber, the railroad subsidiary of WVP&P Co. from 1901 to 1910, to serve as the Company doctor at Spruce, following his marriage to Laura Susanna Bock. Dr. Arbuckle's departure from Cass in 1914 enabled Dr. Hannah to become the Company doctor at Cass. He and his family quickly moved there, where he purchased Dr. Arbuckle's house and office, which were built close to the hospital. The town of Cass, as well as WVP&P Co., gained an extremely capable and devoted doctor in this move.

In addition to his duties as Company doctor, he also developed an extensive private practice throughout the town and countryside. This being the era of doctors making housecalls, he was extremely busy visiting the sick and delivering babies in the homes, in addition to serving loggers and employees throughout the entire WVP&P Co. logging domain. He provided outstanding and dedicated service to all for over 29 years, until his death in October 1943.

When the Smallpox vaccination was developed in 1923, Dr. Hannah attempted to vaccinate all persons in Cass. The result was that there was only one Smallpox death that year; a great relief to the community as a whole.

Doctor's fees were deducted monthly from the employee's pay at the rate of $0.75 for single employees and $1.00 for those with families. This paid for all services rendered by the doctor for the month. The doctor also dispensed certain medications directly, with prescriptions being filled at the pharmacy within the Company Store.

A town building containing the Mayor's office, a council meeting room, and a four cell brick walled jail was eventually constructed. For fire fighting, the Company constructed a reservoir on top of the hill on the west side of town. It was connected to an extensive network of "valve houses" at the saw mill and throughout the Company owned portion of the town.

A pedestrian wire suspension bridge across the Greenbrier River to East Cass was constructed in 1901, located adjacent to the site of the later vehicular bridges.

The year 1902 was especially memorable to both the residents and owners of early Cass. In January, the WVP&P Co. saw mill made its first cut. In June the first moves were taken toward the incorporation of Cass as a town within the state of West Virginia. By August 3rd all relevant legal requirements, including an independent survey of the geographic boundaries of Cass, were complete. The certification of more than 100 people qualifying as voting residents living in Cass

was also satisfied. A referendum and its results, 39 votes for incorporation and 2 against, was held. The Board of Elections of Pocahontas County formally approved the Incorporation election results. August 15th, 1902 marks the date that Cass was no longer an unincorporated village, but a legally recognized Incorporated Town in the state of West Virginia. It was no longer so much a state of mind but rather a tangible entity.

In a move that smacks of biting the hand that feeds you, the Cass Town Council condemned the Company bridge in September 1902 for not being equipped with wires along its sides for pedestrian railings. The Company promptly added these to the bridge in late 1902. This swinging bridge served until 1908 when it was replaced by a single lane steel through truss bridge built by the State. In 1917-1918 construction began on a two lane concrete arch bridge, which is still in use today. This bridge, which was

Prior to the construction of the steel bridge at Cass in 1908, horses and wagons had to ford the Greenbrier River, as shown here. The relatively shallow water near the mouth of Leatherbark Creek led to the previously undeveloped area being known as Leatherbark Ford. (Photographer unknown, West Virginia and Regional History Collection, West Virginia University Libraries)

False work forms to support the arches of the concrete bridge under construction at Cass were placed upstream of the existing steel bridge in this 1918 vintage photo. (Photographer unknown, collection of Pocahontas County Historical Society)

"officially" completed in 1920, was required to handle the ever increasing volume of both pedestrian and vehicular traffic.

Early in 1903, the entire town of Cass had the unpaved streets lined with wooden boardwalks, such that tenants and visitors no longer had to walk in the dirt streets, which were often muddy or icy. Main Street was paved with river rocks dug by hand in 1932. Aside from the construction of the homes themselves, the Company continued to erect or convert structures to different uses as their need became apparent. The Company built a Masonic Lodge Hall on Front Street which has been in continual use throughout Cass' existence. In addition, the Company supported several places of worship, including the Cass Presbyterian Church on Front Street, which now functions as the Cass Community Center ,and the Methodist Church (now interdenominational) at the corner of Spruce and "A" Street. A meeting hall for the Odd Fellows was constructed on Main Street, south of the Company

owned properties. The first floor was used as a 5 & 10 cent store and later an independent grocery store. This store was last operated by Jack Kane, well into the 1980's.

"Slabtown"

WVP & P Co. constructed a tanning and dye extract plant south of Cass below Cold Run in 1913-1914. This facility operated under the name of Industrial Chemical Company of New York, but was usually referred to by residents as the "Extract Plant". To provide housing for extract plant employees 11 houses were built on a single street just north of, and parallel to, the banks of Cold Run. It was south of the southern border of the incorporated town of Cass. These houses were similar in appearance to the Class Three Houses in Cass. They were supplied with electricity by the Company. However, water was supplied by hand pumps and from shallow wells. There was no inside plumbing in these houses when originally built. Arthur

Looking east from the hillside above the Greenbrier River, the business district of East Cass can be seen at center, "Dirty Street" extended north from the bridge at left, and the single story houses in "colored bottom" can be seen between the thick groves of trees at the right edge. (Photographer unknown, Vladimir Maleckar Collection, West Virginia State Archives)

Moulton, superintendent of the Extract Plant, occupied the largest of these houses.

This area became known as "Slabtown", apparently because the boardwalks outside of the houses were made with the outer cut from logs. These were not sawed flat on the outer surface and were known as slabs. The Extract Plant was closed in 1928 and burned in 1930, but some of the Slabtown houses were occupied into the late 1980's. The remaining houses are no longer occupied. The current Fire and Rescue Building sits close to the northern edge of Slabtown.

Bohunk Hill

North of the managers' houses on "Big Bug Hill" was a small, unplanned gathering of rudely constructed houses, sheds, and barns. Known as Bohunk Hill, it was apparently started by the immigrant railroad builders. Located close to the junction of the C&O and the logging railroad, it was convenient to their work activities. It was physically seperated from the Company Town, but ultimately was included within the Cass corporate limits. It provided a sheltered, diversified community for the immigrant workers at Cass who may not have been fluent in the English language. As a result, they usually had lower paying jobs in the logging operations and a lower economic status. Although many were proud Eastern European descendants, making a living in the English-speaking community was difficult. They made do with whatever they could and contributed their own energy to the growth of Cass.

East Cass

The Incorporation of the town of Cass included the Company houses and structures built on the west side of the Greenbrier River, as well as a similar sized area east of the river. East Cass, sometimes referred to as Brooklyn, consisted of privately owned dwellings, a bustling business district, and an area known as "colored bottom". The Company provided ten single story houses south of the East Cass business district for use by black employees.

East Cass has declined significantly and the establishments on "Dirty Street" have disappeared in this April 1974 photo taken from the hillside behind the Company Store. (Photo by George A. Fizer)

These 16 foot by 25 foot wood frame houses had six foot deep porches both on the front and the rear. Built with only two rooms and no chimney, the stovepipe exited through the walls, resulting in several fires through the years. A fuel shed and outhouse were behind each house. The rental rate was $2.50 per month.

In addition, there was a Company owned vegetable garden and a pesthouse located in the southern portion of the Company owned section of the river bottom. John Slavin, and later Charlie Sheets, had large gardens on this land for many years.

Initially East Cass had one street, through the river bottom, and Greenbank Road close to the hillside. There were only a few individual dwellings, including at least one dwelling that predated the founding of Cass.

Two large areas of privately owned land were south of the town line; the Allen E. Burner Annex, along Greenbank Road, and the Blackhurst Addition, which was south and west of the Burner Annex. The Blackhurst Addition was partially bounded by Greenbank Road (WV Route 66), the Burner Annex on the east, and the Greenbrier River to the west. The owners of both of these properties auctioned, or otherwise sold off, portions of their land to others who

wanted their own homes or didn't desire living in the Company Town. The auction of The Blackhurst Addition was held May 26, 1915. Newspaper accounts relate there was a brass band and twenty dollars in gold given away. The auctioneer was Captain C.B. Swecker and the sale agent was American Co. of Charleston, WV. Current tax maps indicate some 52 lots were associated with the Burner Annex and another 47 were from the Blackhurst Addition. This entire area was typically referred to as "The Blackhurst Addition". Originally these houses did not have electricity or indoor plumbing.

Due to the rapidly growing population in The Blackhurst Addition, in December 1915 a 200 foot long swinging bridge was built to provide access from this portion of East Cass to a point near the southern boundary of the Company Town. Built by William M. Siple and Sons, it was rather substantial. It included continuous side screening and 1" by 10" longitudinal floor boards laid lengthwise on top of the wooden 2"by 8" spruce cross pieces connecting the two sides. In addition, there was 140 feet of elevated walkway extending from the west end of the bridge to the west side of the railroad track embankment. While the Company provided cables, lumber, wire, and other

The houses built in the Burner Annex and the Blackhurst Addition, as seen through a telephoto lens from the hillside to the west of the Greenbrier River, show the diversity of size, shape, and orientation of these privately owned residences. The additions stretched from the north (above) to the south (below) along "Greenbank Road" which is identified as First Avenue on the current county tax maps. (Both photos by Ivan O. Clarkson, collection of Sonny Burruss)

The two room houses in the area known as "colored bottom" as seen in the early 1970's provided minimal shelter for the residents. (Photo by George A. Fizer)

Shorty's Restaurant, Cass, W. Va.

Post cards were an inexpensive means of correspondance. This one shows the interior of the restaurant in East Cass that was run by Shorty Brill in the building next to the bridge at Cass. (Photographer unknown, collection of Pocahontas County Historical Society)

building materials for both the construction and maintenance of the bridge, repairs were performed by community members. During anything more than minor flooding of the Greenbrier River, occupants of The Blackhurst Addition had to walk north to the main road and use that bridge for access to Cass in order to go to work, to school, or to attend services in any of the churches located on the west side of the river. When the floodwaters were high, as during the spring ice melts, several of the homes in East Cass were completely cut off from Cass, except for the foot bridge.

The "Blackhurst Addition" added individual residences, several of which housed family-run convenience stores and bars in later years.

The East Cass business district had several notable structures including mercantile stores run by Max Curry and Jacob Cooper. Close to the river and south of the bridge was Shorty Brill's Restaurant which was later run as a bar by Charlie Gum. By 1924 there were at least 30 business other than WVP&P Co. operating in Cass.

The stories of raucous woodsmen returning to East Cass have truth to them. North of the business area and along the east side of the river was an area of bars, gaming houses, and brothels. It was known then, and continues to be known as "Dirty Street".

Built along the river bottom, or flood plain, all these areas east of the Greenbrier River were subject to periodic, and sometimes severe, flooding. While many undated vintage photos show significant high water and floods, Greenbrier River floods in 1985 and 1995 washed away almost all the remnants of the East Cass Business district, the "colored bottom", and the structures along the river front. All that remains of "Dirty Street" is the abandoned structure of the River View Hotel, a notorious destination for woodsmen when they visited Cass.

Because of the pollution of the Greenbrier River, due to the discharge of raw sewage into it from the buildings of Cass on both sides of the river, the town swimming hole was just south of The Blackhurst Addition at "Blackhurst's Bottom". At this point Deer Creek flowed into the Greenbrier River from the east. A large and fairly deep body of fresh water accumulated there before it continued its flow into the Greenbrier. It was a favorite summer place for the youngsters!

Some of the establishments on "Dirty Street" north of the bridge in East Cass. Today the River View Hotel is the only structure still in existence, but it stands unused. (Photographer unknown, West Virginia and Regional History Collection, West Virginia University Libraries)

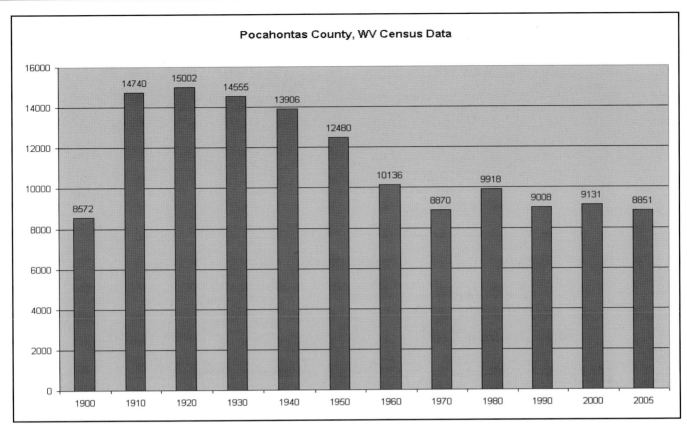

Pocahontas County, WV Census Data

U.S. Census data from 1900 to 2000 for Pocahontas County, WV mirrors the fortunes of the operations at Cass. (Data courtesy U.S. Department of Interior, presentation by Catherine S. Futej)

In 1916 Charles Luke married Elizabeth Hannah, the youngest daughter of Mr. and Mrs. S.B. Hannah of Arbovale. They built a summer residence at Cass, which became a place for the WVP&P Co. upper management to use for business and social gatherings in the beautiful mountains of West Virginia. Known locally as "The Clubhouse", by 1918 the house was enlarged and was occupied by the Company Superintendent at Cass, E.P. Shaffer, along with his wife and growing family.

By then, World War I was already devastating parts of Europe. With the United States' growing involvement, a significant number of residents from Cass and other towns in Pocahontas County joined the military services. The war demands caused the saw mill business to grow dramatically and Cass continued to mature as a town. The Company purchased additional land and structures in East Cass, which served to stabilize the economy. At the same time it put a tighter constriction on "Dirty Street" activities by providing a physical buffer zone between that area and the homes, schools, and places of employment for the Cass residents.

By 1920, Cass and its associated operations had reached a peak. The mill was now running two 11-hour shifts, six days a week. The Extract Plant was running full time. The Company had built over 400 structures in Cass and its surrounding area. The official town census showed 1195 residents in the incorporated town of Cass. Based on unofficial counts, property auction records, county deeds, and some estimates done on the basis of the ratio of WVP&P Co. employees and the population included in the incorporated town census, there were approximately 900 additional people living predominantly south of the incorporated town on both sides of the river. A well understood social structure existed, and although not set down by law, the town was divided by residents' employee class and cultural diversity.

Unlike many communities, Cass never had a "town" cemetery; though there are a multitude of family owned plots scattered throughout the area and at one time there was a potter's field cemetery. This land, on the northwest side of Cass, was adjacent to the Company Pasture. Several acres of what had been the Company's pastureland were later cleared by the Civilian Conservation Corp. (CCC) to be used as a ball field and for other recreational activities. The unidentified individuals were disinterred and reburied at the cemetery near Deer Creek.

In the early 1920's the automobile reached Cass in sufficient number for a fuel tank to be installed near the Company Store for resale purposes. In June 1923, the C&O agreed to replace their small original station with a larger, more modern one, which was in service by September. By February 1926, continuous telegraph service commenced between Marlinton and Durbin, with an operator on duty at Cass for each of two eight-hour shifts.

While the lumber business was still holding extremely well, a portent of things to come occurred when the Extract Plant was closed, dismantled, and sold to scrappers and used equipment purveyors in 1928. All of the employees were laid off, though a few may have found other work within WVP&P Co.'s lumbering business.

The era from 1901 to 1920 was a time of continuous growth at Cass and all of Pocahontas County. The population expanded rapidly until the "Great Depression" of the 1930's. The poor worldwide economic conditions reduced the demand for wood products from the saw mill.

Business began to slow dramatically in the late-1920's. Soon after, the "Great Depression" stuck and unemployment became rampant. Residents of Cass were in a better situation than those in many other places, since virtually all of the dwellings, including the Company houses, had room for a garden. Many residents had a cow or two and these were allowed to graze on the Company Pasture for a small monthly fee. Residents of the east side of the Greenbrier River took to driving their cows to the property of the old Extract Plant for grazing. Many residents also raised hogs for butchering and chickens for both eggs and meat throughout the year. The mid-1920's was also a time of the silent motion picture, which had quite a following in Cass. Starting in the early 1920's and continuing concurrently with the growth of the motion picture industry was the presentation of silent films, followed by the "talkies", to the residents of Cass and its surrounding areas.

The brutal beginning of the full-blown depression began on October 24, 1929 with the Stock

The former undertaker's house in East Cass continues in use today as The Cass Inn, a bed and breakfast, for tourists. (Photo by George A. Fizer)

Even Cass couldn't avoid the sales and marketing expertise of Henry Ford. Baxter Auto Sales in East Cass, south on Greenbank Road from the bridge, was the authorized Ford dealer. (Photographer unknown, West Virginia and Regional History Collection, West Virginia University Libraries)

Market Crash. This had the almost immediate effect of the Company Mill dropping the second shift completely and cutting back its hours of operation. In addition, the Company could no longer afford to keep Doctor Cofer stationed at Slaty Fork to provide medical services to employees there or at Bergoo. Hence, Dr. Hannah would drive there two days a week, once the CCC road was finished. Prior to that time, either Dr. Cofer was there on call, or Dr. Hannah rode a log train to Slaty Fork and back.

For many families in Cass, the reality of the Depression was heart-rendering, especially for those without a garden or livestock. Mack H. Brooks, principal of the school, set up a free lunch program to help those most in need. Persons who were employed by the Company, or otherwise working, supplied beans, vegetables, and bread. Many of the more prosperous residents took turns providing a meat dish. The ninth graders helped prepare and serve the food.

1930 was also the year of one of the worst droughts in memory in Pocahontas County. While WVP&P Co. managed to suppress and prevent fires fairly successfully, hundreds of men from Cass and

Durbin left to help fight fires along the Western Maryland Railroad.

Floodwaters again did great damage to East Cass businesses in 1932, as well as to many of the homes there. In addition, great damage was done to the cement bridge across the river, which resulted in the northern half of the bridge at the East Cass end collapsing and falling into the river. The Pocahontas Construction Company was placed in charge of replacing the destroyed portion of the bridge. They did such a good job that it has withstood all subsequent floods. A small number of Cass residents also got some employment working on the bridge repair. Some residents remarked that nature seemed determined to permanently erase "Dirty Street" from existence.

In 1933 the CCC opened a camp, named Camp Randolph, at the top of Cold Run where it met Back Mountain Road. This camp provided work for significant numbers of youth in the Cass area. For approximately two years they toiled to build a road over the southeastern portion of Cheat Mountain to the town of Linwood, which is slightly south of where

The Company Houses at Cass were built on 50 foot by 100 foot lots which allowed the residents to cultivate their own gardens as shown here behind the houses on Spruce Street. (Phil Bagdon Collection, West Virginia State Archives)

Snowshoe Resort is today. (This road did not get paved for another 60+ years.)

While Cass fared a bit better than many small towns as the Company attempted to always keep some folks employed in the woods, on the railroad, or in the mills, in 1934 there was a three-month strike, brought about primarily by unrest caused by the depression and exacerbated by the talk of unionization.

Life in Cass settled into an uncertain existence for most families, working when they could, growing as much food as possible themselves, and bartering with friends and neighbors for services and things they needed but couldn't afford. In 1933 E.P. Shaffer retired due to seriously declining health. According to fellow employees and contemporary Cass residents, his health had been quite poor since 1928.

Since the founding of Cass, the papermaking technology of WVP&P Co. had advanced dramatically. The development of new paper making techniques, which used fast growing "loblolly" pine as a source for pulpwood, reduced the need to harvest spruce from Cheat Mountain. Mr. Shaffer's retirement is believed to have been a significant impetus for the decision to log certain areas that still had high value, extremely saleable lumber and this accelerated the Company

decision to sell the whole West Virginia Operation. As the logging activities slowed people looked elsewhere for income and gradually many moved away.

Corporate and personal financial situations began to see some small, but noticeable, improvement in the later 1930's. The West Penn Electric Company made plans in December 1936 to extended their electric supply lines from Marlinton to Durbin, with an extension from Dunmore to Cass. By summer of 1937, residents of the southern part of East Cass, privately owned homes in West Cass, and surrounding farms and communities all had the satisfaction of electric lighting.

Unfortunately there were several deaths within the ranks of WVP&P Co.'s upper management; some of which, no doubt, effected the future of the Cass operations. In 1934 David Luke, President of WVP&P Co. died of a heart attack. His son Alexander, who had lived in Cass during the 1927-29 period, passed away in May of the same year. In November 1938, Joseph Cass died. Although he had been a Director of the Company for more than 30 years, he was not well-known by the residents and his death passed with little local recognition. In 1939 Charles W. Luke passed away at age 51. He was an extremely involved, proactive, Vice President at the time of his death.

As the Depression eased and Europe was virtually a tinderbox on the brink of exploding, American industry began to grow again. Orders began growing in increasing volume for all type of materials. European Allies, primarily England, and the U.S. Government ordered materials and supplies for the European war which seemed to be inevitable. With the institution of the mandatory draft, this growth had an unexpected affect on Cass life. Many families had left and moved to industrial cities like Baltimore and Pittsburgh, where war-related jobs were growing in volume. A significant number of the residents were drafted, and after the attack on Pearl Harbor, enlisting in the military increased.

During this time WVP&P Co. had firmly decided to completely dispose of all the timber land leases and rights, all of the logging operations, the railroad and wood processing infrastructure, and all of the ownership in Cass. While the administrative, marketing, contractual, and legal activities actually did not happen instantaneously, they were handled in a discrete but expeditious manner. In less than two years from America's entry into World War II in 1941, the entire transaction was completed. On August 20, 1943 all WVP&P Co.'s holding, including the timberlands, mill, and Cass itself, were sold to the Mower Lumber Company. It seems that the sale came as a surprise to most of the residents, although there had been rumors to the effect that something of the sort was bound to happen. If one were superstitious, the death of E.P. Shaffer in February 1943 might have been taken as a harbinger of the sale.

The Mower Lumber Company

The Mower Lumber Company was owned and operated by Roger Donald Mower and Frank Edwin Mower, descendants of Irwin Maurer who migrated from Altoona, Pennsylvania to Ingrid, West Virginia in the late 1800's. He was a railroad man. He started as telegraph operator and became General Manager of the Dry Fork Railroad. He married into the Hickman family of Hendricks, West Virginia. The Hickman's were involved in logging operations at Timber, West Virginia where the Mower brothers would work with their uncles, the Hickman's, during the summer. After completing college they began to acquire saw mills in West Virginia. Apparently they had a knack for buying struggling operations and bringing them back to life.

Working from offices in the family home in Charleston, they purchased the operations at Cass in 1943, but railroad records indicate they operated at Cass beginning in June of 1942. Interestingly, their grandmother's relatives had settled in Pocahontas County near Knapp's Creek, south of Marlinton. In fact, the Company Store Manager, Mr. Hickman was a cousin of the mother of Donald and Edwin.

The Company Farm was sold to Edwin's wife, Dorothy. She renamed it PocaDot Farm. She raised race horses and the racing silks were green and white, which resulted in the farm buildings being painted white with light green trim.

Among the first visible changes in the town was that Nethken's Meat Market building, adjacent to the Company Store, became the Post Office since the Mowers moved their offices into the post office space in the Company Store. The Pocahontas Supply Company ceased to exist and the store building's interior was redone. The Mowers had all of the Company houses repainted, supplied minor maintenance as required, rebuilt the wooden boardwalks, and installed picket fences around each Company owned home in town. Since all of the buildings, fences, and boardwalks were painted white, the town regained its vibrant, and almost elegant, image.

However, the ambiance at Cass was significantly different after the end of the war. Large numbers of the residents and their families had become familiar with the world outside of Cass. They experienced the life style choices and economic opportunities it had to offer. Many former residents, who left Cass out of economic necessity, chose to remain in the large cities they initially moved to for the employment opportunities they represented near the end of the depression and during the war years. Significant numbers of young men, returning from military service, took advantage of their veteran's benefits to attend colleges and other facilities of higher education. The mindset of the population was no longer what it had been for nearly a half-century. No longer were all the residents satisfied with life in a rural town.

While the Mower Lumber Company continued its operations throughout the immediate postwar years and through the 1950's, both the volume of business and the accessibility of high quality lumber for harvest

Frank Edwin Mower (l) and Donald Roger Mower (r), the owners of the Mower Lumber Company acquired the Cass operations from WVP&P Co. in 1943. Donald continued the operation after Edwin's death in 1956 and finally closed it on July 1, 1960. (Both photos West Virginia and Regional History Collection, West Virginia University Libraries)

were continually declining. The resulting economic hardship and uncertainty affected all of the residents, since without the lumber industry, Cass, like many Company towns, would essentially have no economic infrastructure left to justify its existence.

In contrast to the planned development of Cass by the Luke family, starting in 1899, and the continued use by the Mower family, starting in 1943, the closing of the operation was rather abrupt and unexpected. The president of Mower Lumber Company, Frank Edwin Mower, passed away in 1956. His brother Donald Roger Mower Sr. continued to operate the business until July 1, 1960 when the last log was sawed and the saw mill whistle blew for the last time.

An interview with Donald's son, Roger Mower Jr. provided the following description of the events that followed:

"The Mower Lumber Company sold all its former Cass area holdings, with exception of the Cass town area and its structures, to J. Peter Grace in 1960. The Grace purchase included the trade name "Mower Lumber Company", which Mr. Grace continued to use with his operation of the timber land, timber tracts, and operational agreements.

With this 1960 sale to Grace, Donald R. Mower organized the "Don Mower Lumber Company", a corporation, to own and operate the remaining Cass property, which included the closed saw mill.

When the State of West Virginia purchased the present day Cass Scenic Railroad the State acquired railroad property, land, the right-of-way, and equipment from both the Mower Lumber Company, owned by Grace, and the Don Mower Lumber Company. At that time, Donald R. Mower attempted to get the State to purchase the entire remaining Cass properties, including both the town and the saw mill. However the State was not interested. After 1960, the Don Mower Lumber Company continued to rent the Cass dwellings and other structures to interested persons seeking to use them. Don Mower Lumber Company also continued to operate the town's water system. House rent was set to an individual's ability to pay, seeking to rent to year-round interest renters. Free paint was supplied, then, to any such renter, who agreed to paint their dwelling.

My father, Donald R. Mower died in 1964 and we attempted to keep his Cass "best intentions" alive.

At that time a Florida resident became interested in the Cass saw mill, with a stated intention of reopening the mill operation using Federal and State aid. In 1966, the Don Mower Lumber Company sold all the Cass properties, including the saw mill, town, and the Don Mower Lumber Company trade name to Mr. J. W. Harrell. The only exception was one dwelling house, which I retained and used as "a cabin" for Cass area visits. Everything else was sold to Mr. Harrell.

He continued to rent houses and structures using the name of Don Mower Lumber Company. During this time, the conditions of the remaining structures began to decline and other town problems began to arise. Mr. Harrell retained some of the former Don Mower Lumber Company employees, as well as the company's attorney. All this gave rise to many area people thinking that I, and the Mower family, were still involved with the Cass town management and ownership. This was especially true since I did retain the one house and made frequent visits to Cass. However, all of the other property was under the ownership and control of Mr. Harrell in Florida. At that time his company, the Don Mower Lumber Company, owned the town of Cass and operated it -

with the exception of the house I reserved from the sale. Neither I, nor any other Mower family member, had any other ownership or interest in the remaining Cass properties."

The closing of the Mower Lumber Company was a terrible blow to the residents and economy of Cass. No other large employer existed in the area. Some folks found work at the National Radio Astronomy Observatory at Greenbank. Others began commuting to the Howes Leather Company tannery at Frank, near Durbin. Many young adults made the difficult decision to leave Cass, and sometimes West Virginia, completely. The Cass population shrank to a shadow of its former size.

The Pocahontas County Deed Books show that the State of West Virginia ultimately came to the rescue in June of 1962 when the railroad shops, the railroad line to Bald Knob, and more than 100 acres at Bald Knob were purchased from the Mower Lumber Company. The Cass Scenic Railroad began operations that year and transient tourist trade has been the economic staple since then. On Demcember 27, 1976 the State was able to purchase 116 acres within the corporate limits of Cass, most of the former Company

Looking north up Main Street at Cass. The number of cars on the street gives the impression the houses are reasonably well occupied. (Photo by Ivan O.Clarkson, collection of Sonny Burruss)

The East Cass business district can be seen behind Western Maryland Shay No. 6 (c/n 3354) at the Cass Depot in May 1981. (Photo by George A. Fizer)

Town of Cass. But that only procured the properties and the houses; funds for stabilization and restoration of the buildings themselves has always been difficult to secure. The use of many of the houses as tourist rental units has helped to ease that problem. The theory says that rental income can help with restoration of more buildings, which in turn can be rented. It's still a formidable task to stave off the natural process of deterioration of the buildings. Just consider what goes into the maintenance of the 65 major structures that remain in the Company Town.

While the Cass Scenic Railroad State Park has continued to preserve the logging and railroad history at the junction of Leatherbark Creek and the Greenbrier River, it hasn't been easy. During the 1970's several of the Company Houses, the saw mill, and the prominent railroad structures were destroyed by deliberately set fires.

The business area of East Cass and virtually all the houses along the east side of the river were destroyed by flood waters on November 5, 1985. Torrential rainfall, reported to be as much as 14 inches in the headwaters of the Greenbrier River, swept over "Dirty Street", the main street at the bridge, and the flood

plain downriver. Many longtime residents lost all their belongings when their houses were destroyed. Some were unable to contact their relatives for as much as three days. The resulting loss of property and decrease in population sadly led to Cass losing its incorporated status. It continues to survive, dependent largely on the State Park.

In August of 2002 the Centennial of the Cass Incorporation was celebrated at the State Park; attended by descendants of the Luke family, Roger Mower, his wife Catherine, and representatives of the State. More recently a few new businesses have sprouted near the bridge in East Cass. Dependant upon the tourist trade generated by the State Park, this may be the resurgance of Cass as it counts toward its second hundred years.

The site of the former East Cass business district as seen from the steps of the Company Store in October 1990. (Photo by George A. Fizer)

Looking north on Main Street at Cass. The restored Company Houses of the Cass Scenic Railroad State Park are ready for tenants on May 18, 2006. (Photo by Gerald M. Futej)

GRADED
SCHOOL

COMPANY
TOWN

MASONIC
LODGE
HALL

BAKER
HOUSE
HOTEL

LOGGERS'
HOTEL

COOPER'S
STORE

SHORTY
BRILL'S

STE
BRID

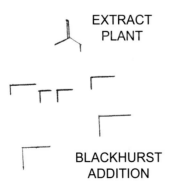

EXTRACT
PLANT

"SLABTOWN"

COLORED
BOTTOM

BLACKHURST
ADDITION

At a Special Term of the Circuit Court of Pocahontas
County, West Virginia, held at the Court House thereof on the
15th. day of August, 1902, the following order was entered of
record:

IN THE MATTER OF THE INCORPORATION OF CASS:

A certificate under oath of Chas. A. Fletcher, Jas. K.
Jackson and harry J. Scott, was this day filed showing that a
majority of all the qualified voters residing in the following
boundary, to-wit: Beginning at an apple tree at the south end
of the lumber dock 65 feet from the center of the railroad S.
81-45 E 200 feet to a white oak on the bank of the River by a
large red oak, N. 73 E 390 feet crossing the River to a red oak
above the County road corner to the lands of Allen E. Burner and
with his line, S 60-30 E 470 feet to two chestnut saplings,
Burner's Corner, continued same course 198 feet to a stake S 41-30
W 1925 feet to a stake S 60-30 E 198 feet to a leaning chestnut
on side of a ridge, N 88 W 720 feet to a stake in a bottom, thence
about N 35 W 2542 feet to a stake, N. 50 E 3250 feet to a stake
on Leather Bark Creek, thence down the same about S 35 E 960 feet
to a sugar in the bottom of said creek S 7-30 W 1180 feet to a
stake 21 feet from the center of railroad on the east side of
said railroad S 30 W 850 feet to a stake S 55-30 E 27 feet to
the point of beginning, containing 162 acres; have been given in
due form of law in favor of the incorporation of the Town of Cass,
in the County of Pocahontas, bounded as herein set forth, And it
appearing to the satisfaction of the Court that all the provisions
of Chapter 47 in Code of West Virginia, have been complied with
by the applicants for said corporation, the said town is duly
authorized within the corporate limits aforesaid to exercise
all the corporate powers conferred by said chapter from and
after the date of a certificate of incorporation which the

At a Special Term of the Circuit Court of Pocahontas
County, West Virginia, held at the Court House thereof on the
15th. day of August, 1902, the following order was entered of
record:

IN THE MATTER OF THE INCORPORATION OF CASS:

A TRUE COPY

TESTE:

D. C. Adkison
Clerk.

By *Geraldine Heust*
Deputy Clerk.

Form No. 10-300 (REV. (9/77)

UNITED STATES DEPARTMENT OF THE INTERIOR
NATIONAL PARK SERVICE

NATIONAL REGISTER OF HISTORIC PLACES INVENTORY -- NOMINATION FORM

SEE INSTRUCTIONS IN *HOW TO COMPLETE NATIONAL REGISTER FORMS*
TYPE ALL ENTRIES -- COMPLETE APPLICABLE SECTIONS

1 NAME

HISTORIC

AND/OR COMMON

Cass Historic District

2 LOCATION

STREET & NUMBER

Intersection of County Routes 1 and 7   __NOT FOR PUBLICATION

CITY, TOWN   CONGRESSIONAL DISTRICT

Cass   __ VICINITY OF   Second

STATE	CODE	COUNTY	CODE
West Virginia	54	Pocahontas	075

3 CLASSIFICATION

CATEGORY	OWNERSHIP	STATUS	PRESENT USE	
X DISTRICT	__PUBLIC	X OCCUPIED	__AGRICULTURE	X MUSEUM
__BUILDING(S)	__PRIVATE	__UNOCCUPIED	X COMMERCIAL	X PARK
__STRUCTURE	X BOTH	X WORK IN PROGRESS	X EDUCATIONAL	X PRIVATE RESIDENCE
__SITE	PUBLIC ACQUISITION	ACCESSIBLE	X ENTERTAINMENT	X RELIGIOUS
__OBJECT	__IN PROCESS	__YES: RESTRICTED	X GOVERNMENT	__SCIENTIFIC
	__BEING CONSIDERED	X YES: UNRESTRICTED	X INDUSTRIAL	X TRANSPORTATION
		__NO	__MILITARY	__OTHER:

4 OWNER OF PROPERTY

NAME   Multiple Ownership

STREET & NUMBER

CITY, TOWN   STATE
                         __ VICINITY OF

5 LOCATION OF LEGAL DESCRIPTION

COURTHOUSE,
REGISTRY OF DEEDS, ETC.   Pocahontas County Courthouse

STREET & NUMBER   Ninth Street

CITY, TOWN   STATE
          Marlinton   West Virginia

6 REPRESENTATION IN EXISTING SURVEYS

TITLE

DATE
                                    __FEDERAL __STATE __COUNTY __LOCAL

DEPOSITORY FOR
SURVEY RECORDS

CITY, TOWN   STATE

33

(Photo by Gay, Marlinton, WV, collection of Richard Dale)

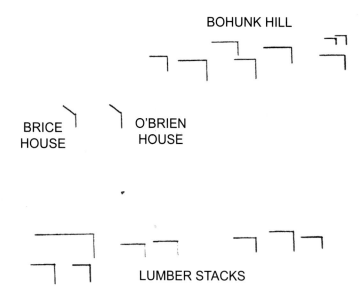

BOHUNK HILL

BRICE
HOUSE

O'BRIEN
HOUSE

LUMBER STACKS

CASS W VA. PHOTO BY CAV 5/15/17

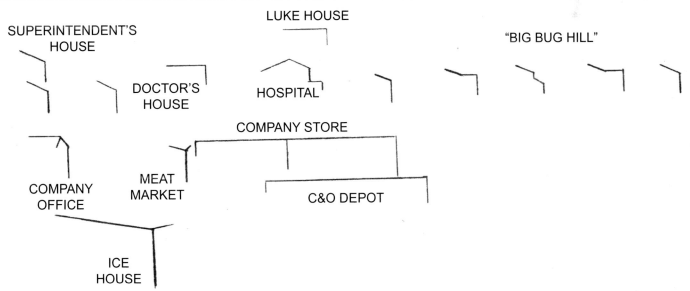

SUPERINTENDENT'S
HOUSE

LUKE HOUSE

"BIG BUG HILL"

DOCTOR'S
HOUSE

HOSPITAL

COMPANY STORE

COMPANY
OFFICE

MEAT
MARKET

C&O DEPOT

ICE
HOUSE

Located on the hillside behind the railroad depot at Cass, the Pocahontas Supply Company store provided food, clothing, and supplies for the town of Cass, to the left, and the logging operations of WVP&P Co. reached by the railroad out of the photo to the right. The narrow two story building immediately to the left of the Company Store was used by the S.B. Nethken & Company Meat Market. ca 1925 (Photographer unknown, collection of William Sampson)

The Company Store at Cass

by Roy B. Clarkson & Gerald M. Futej

The Pocahontas Supply Company

Starting a new business venture in the mountain wilderness was a real challenge. The Luke family and the managers of the West Virginia Pulp & Paper Company (WVP&P Co.) provided the land, the hardware, and the equipment for harvesting the timber on Cheat Mountain. They depended upon rugged individuals to provide the necessary manpower to utilize those resources. The lumberjacks, known as wood hicks, train crews, and mill workers toiled long hours under sometimes trying conditions. While the Company town of Cass provided shelter for many, they still needed food and clothing in order to survive. Before the coming

of the Chesapeake and Ohio Railroad (C&O), transportation in Pocahontas County was by foot, horseback, or wagon. Some of the first workers employed at Cass came with their families by wagon train. They carried their belongings with them. Preserved food, clothing, and other personal needs came by wagon over Allegheny Mountain from Virginia and Maryland.

Hunting, trapping, gardening, and berry picking in their spare time couldn't possibly sustain the workers or the families of those that accompanied them to Cass. When Cass was established, shopping malls and convenience stores were decades in the future.

However, it was the practice of lumber and coal mining companies, when establishing a new industry in a sparsely inhabited area, to open a store where workers could buy supplies. These were universally called the "Company Store".

When the Luke family began their operations at Cass, one of the first things they did was to open a store. In June 1900 they established the Pocahontas Supply Company, a subsidiary of West Virginia Pulp and Paper Company, with a capital stock of ten thousand dollars. The Pocahontas Supply Company initially provided food and supplies for the builders of the logging railroad at Cass. Later, it sent food via the logging railroad to supply the cooks who prepared meals for the loggers at the camps on the mountains. As the saw mill started operation, more skilled workers arrived at Cass and many brought their families with them. The Company built homes for many of them but this population explosion in the wilderness demanded more supplies. With the increasing numbers of families there was a need to provide more than just food, clothing, and housing. Household goods, furniture, and building supplies were needed to sustain the growing community.

The Pocahontas Supply Company started business in a two story gabled roof building constructed on the rise just above the Greenbrier River at Cass, right below the site of the houses of the managers of the West Virginia Pulp & Paper Company. The first store was built in 1900. Under Robert S. Hickman, manager from 1902 to 1947, the Pocahontas Supply Company store became one of the largest Company Stores in the country.

One of the biggest problems in the early days was providing fresh meat. The Company owned its own farm along Deer Creek and raised most of the cattle and hogs that were used. Beef was slaughtered at a slaughter house located near the present locomotive shop. The preparation and selling of meat was handled by S.B. Nethken and Company, whose market was located adjacent to the main store.

It was easy to take care of poultry; chickens and turkeys were kept in a pen north of the store. Customers picked the bird they wanted. It was then caught; its legs were tied, and it was handed to the customer who did her own preparation.

The store at Cass served as the entire operation until the early teens. By then a more spacious salesroom for the south end of the store was needed. But the proximity of the Nethken Meat Market was an impediment. The resourceful Company managers simply relocated the meat market, approximately 30 feet, to the south. The original building was set on a new foundation. Later the telephone exchange was installed upstairs. With the meat market moved, the salesroom was enlarged and the roof was changed to a flat sloped roof. The new salesroom facade sported a central entrance doorway and a total of four second floor windows equally spaced across the front. Warehouse space to the north was provided as well as the salesroom and showroom space.

In 1905, a branch store was opened at the new town of Spruce, WV. Later branches were also opened at Cheat Bridge, Laurel Bank, and Bemis.

For more than twenty years ice was cut on the Greenbrier River and stored in a 35 foot by 45 foot ice house that was insulated with a one-foot thick layer of sawdust. This would last until mid summer. The ice house was located near the river at the west end of the present bridge.

Fire was always the greatest fear for the lumbermen. Everywhere they turned there was a bountiful supply of fuel just waiting to be ignited. Fear turned to reality at the Pocahontas Supply Company on March 19, 1918, when a portion of the building was damaged by fire. Newspaper reports at the time recount the sale of smoke and water damaged merchandise, a real "fire sale"!

Rather than rebuild in kind, the Pocahontas Supply Company chose to enlarge the building. The meat market to the south of the building was once again moved. Mechanical refrigeration equipment was installed in the basement to provide cooling for the meat. A year-round source for ice was provided by an ice machine located behind the meat market.

In addition to the southern expansion a third floor was added. The resulting building facade had two rows of eight windows across the front. The entrance door was also relocated to the south between the fifth and sixth windows. Apparently, at the same time the warehouse space to the north of the salesroom was expanded. It was lengthened and raised to three stories with a full basement. A 3000 pound capacity freight elevator was installed to help with the movement of products between the floors. Built by the Craig Ridgway & Sons Company of Coatesville, PA; it remains in operation today.

High water on the Greenbrier River attracted local residents to the original swinging bridge, built in 1901. In the background are the two story buildings used by the Pocahontas Supply Company and the Nethken Meat Market. The lack of railings on the bridge dates this photo before the end of 1902. It's interesting to note that the apparently unpainted Company Store structures predate the managers' houses yet to be built on the hill behind them. (Photographer unknown, collection of Pocahontas County Historical Society)

Taken from the hillside on the East side of the Greenbrier River after the 1908 completion of the single lane steel bridge, this photo clearly shows the original gable roofed Company Store at Cass. The dark two story structure to the right of the store and behind the depot provided housing for the initial WVP&P Co. workers at Cass. The boardwalk alongside the Nethken Meat Market was connected by a stairway to boardwalks leading to the managers' houses on "Big Bug Hill". ca 1910 (Photographer unknown, collection of Ben Kline, courtesy of Railroad Museum of Pennsylvania)

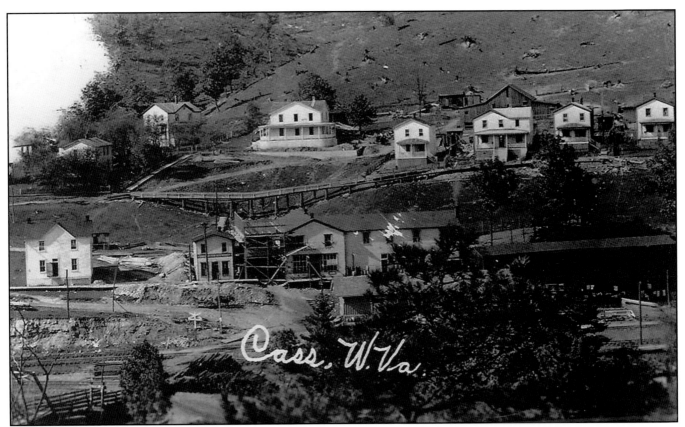

Expansion of the Company Store in the mid-teens required relocation of the meat market. The ungraded soil around the base of the meat market suggests a new foundation, and possibly a basement, was constructed and the building was moved onto it. The new studded walls of the Company Store addition extended above the eaves of the original building in anticipation of a new facade and sloping flat roof. (Photographer unknown, collection of William Sampson)

The renovated Company Store with two story facade and sloping flat roof tended to dwarf the Nethken Meat Market immediately to its left. Notice how the boardwalk to "Big Bug Hill" was relocated well to the south of the meat market, alongside the WVP&P Co. office building, a more direct route from the office building to the Luke House which overlooked the entire area. The railroad trestle, to the right, with the box cars on it, allowed the box cars to be brought directly to the store's warehouse for unloading. (Photo by Gay, Marlinton, WV, collection of Richard Dale)

The main store at Cass was the supermarket of its time. It carried almost every item needed by the workforce, the townspeople, and the surrounding trading area. It sold both dress and work clothes as well as shoes for men, women and children, loggers' boots, fabrics, jewelry, furniture, dishes, household wares, groceries, coal, hay, books, toys, flowers, ice, ice cream, and soda pop. A drug department was located in the store where prescription drugs and a variety of patent medicines could be purchased.

Staples such as canned goods, feed, nails, fencing, and loggers' boots were purchased by the railroad carload. As many as four carloads of condensed milk were purchased at one time. An elevated railroad siding along the east side of the warehouse building allowed for direct unloading of railroad box cars and provided a place to load the supply cars that went to the logging camps. The supply cars, owned by the Company, would be taken to the logging camps when trains went up the mountain to get logs for the saw mill. At one time there was a large north-pointing white arrow painted on the roof to help airplane pilots to check their direction. Selling everything from dog licenses to jewelry; the Pocahontas Supply Company Store had an annual business of over a million dollars for many years. That would be several million in today's dollars.

The enlarged Supply Company building was now 300 feet long by 60 feet wide with a full basement. It included the post office, the pharmacy, an ice cream fountain, and later a short order restaurant. A portion of the addition became the Company payroll office, which was very convenient for both the Company and the employee. The Supply Company sold "on account"

The interior of the Company Store at Cass showed the extent of goods available, from candy to clothing, all in glass cases. The U.S. Post Office counter and postal boxes, to the left, lined the front wall of the store. The inset shows obverse and reverse of script minted for the Pocahontas Supply Company but apparently never issued or used. (Photographer unknown, collection of H.E. Matics, courtesy of Roy B. Clarkson)

The final expansion of the Pocahontas Supply Company store required the meat market to be moved south once again. Notice how close to the WVP&P Co. office building it is here. The warehouse portion, at right, was also expanded, both to the north and to the east, creating the offset in the front facade which exists today. The advent of the automobile brought with it the demand for gasoline which the Supply Company accommodated. (Photographer unknown, collection of William Sampson)

to the employees. Most of the Supply Company business was done on a charge basis. Bills were written on small billing pads which included a carbon copy. Customers were given a copy for their records. The bills of the Company employees were subtracted from the worker's pay each payday. The employees received what was left at the payroll office and since it was right next to the Company Store, they had the opportunity to spend that too before going home. Many lumber and coal companies used script to pay their employees. Script was minted for the Pocahontas Supply Company but never used. It's interesting to note also that contrary to the notion of Company Stores charging exorbitant prices, the Pocahontas Supply Company charged reasonable prices for their goods.

The Company provided food and lodging for the loggers who worked on the mountain. Those wood hicks normally received almost all of their pay in cash,

since they normally didn't have direct access to charge anything at the store. They had a tendency to stay at the camps in the woods, allowing their pay to accumulate. Periodically, the wood hicks would return to town, draw their pay and have a "blow in"; drinking, gambling, and carousing in East Cass, across the Greenbrier River from the Company Store. Many frequented the establishments on "Dirty Street" near the town limits to the north of East Cass. It's been said that "Dirty Street" had all the pleasures a man could want.

On occasion, when wood hicks ran out of money, but weren't ready to return to the woods, they would use the Company credit system as an ATM. A wood hick would buy merchandise on credit from the store, take it outside or across the river, and sell it at a reduced price to replenish his cash. The proceeds were used to continue partying. The cost of that merchandise

Photo of a post card showing the businesses in East Cass across the Greenbrier River. Taken between 1908 and 1918 the sign on Max Curry's store is at left. The tall white building at the left edge is the ice house on the west side of the river. (Photo of postcard by Ivan O. Clarkson, collection of Sonny Burruss)

would be deducted from his next pay, whenever he came back from the woods to collect it. Apparently, the wood hicks would party until the money was spent. Then they would ride the log train back to the logging camp and start the cycle all over again.

In the 1920's a store was established at Slaty Fork. It was operated by Polly and Lyle "Peck" McPherson until 1938 when it closed. The McPherson's returned to Cass where Polly worked as a bookkeeper and clerk at Kane's Store in the southern part of Cass. Peck took work at the sawmill, moving logs in the mill pond.

Bulky items such as feed, hay, coal, and ice were delivered free to townspeople and surrounding farmers. The Company had its own coal mines located along their logging railroad. In the 1930's they delivered coal to the area schools. The coal trucks often got "stuck" in the muddy roads leading to the one room schools around the county.

The "Competition"

Directly across the river from the Company Store was the business district of East Cass. Although

within the incorporated boundary of Cass, most of this area was not part of the West Virginia Pulp & Paper Company holdings.

On the north side of the road just east of the bridge was the mercantile store owned by Max Curry. It was opened before 1908 and continued in operation until 1915. A pair of suspicious fires at the store resulted in Max Curry serving six years for arson. Over time that two story building at the end of the bridge deteriorated and was damaged by floods. By the 1970's no traces of the building could be found.

South of the road, at the end of the bridge, a brick building stood which housed a general store run by "Shorty" Brill. This was later "Buck" Hamrick's pool hall and beer joint. Other establishments along the main street of East Cass included David Finger's General Store which was Finger-Siegel Company by 1917. There were three hotels, several restaurants, and a number of other businesses in East Cass including a theatre and a 5 & 10 cent store. Samuel Cooper's (later Jacob Cooper's) General Store can be seen in photos dating from 1908. It apparently was opened until at least 1924. The businesses in East Cass were

Kane's Grocery Store on Main Street near the south end of Cass. The Class Three House at the left is still in use as a rental cabin by the Cass Scenic Railroad State Park. The warehouse to the right, which was also used as a movie theater, has been removed. (Cass Collection - Rhoda Barb, West Virginia State Archives)

not nearly as stable as the Company Store. Over the years the buildings changed owners, burned, were rebuilt, and were sold again. The business buildings of East Cass eventually succumbed to lack of use following the boom years of the logging operations and the ravages of the Greenbrier River floods.

According to published accounts by former Cass residents, 1939 was a recession year. Apparently as a result of that economic condition John Kane, long time clerk and grocery manager for the Pocahontas Supply Company, found himself unemployed. With a reported capital of just $750.00, he opened a grocery store on the first floor of the Odd Fellows Building on Main Street at the south end of Cass. The Odd Fellows Building was not on property owned by West Virginia Pulp & Paper Company, therefore they had no control over its use.

John's previous employment at the Company Store provided excellent on-the-job training. It's said that he was a hard-nosed negotiator when dealing with salesmen. However, he was a kind-hearted neighbor when giving grocery credit to his customers. His ability to walk a fine economic line was rewarded. He operated Kane's Store and passed it on to his sons, Jack and Ernest "Red", who maintained it in operation until 1987. The declining number of residents at Cass, especially following the flood of 1985, was not enough to support the store financially. However, "Red" still operates the Durbin Mercantile Company (DMC), a grocery store in Durbin.

Two other very small grocery stores apparently served the area as well. Both appear to have been run out of the first floor of individual family residences. John Reda had his store and home near the south end of "Dirty Street". The significance of that location has been lost. Possibly it was a convenience for the residents and "visitors" of that area who might otherwise not be welcome at the more "reputable" stores in Cass. Then again, he may have been open for those clients at hours when the other stores in town were closed. We can only guess.

Construction of the Cooper store in East Cass. Unfortunately the identities of the individuals shown have been lost. Ca 1910 (Photographer unknown, collection of Pocahontas County Historical Society)

East Cass business district following a flood sometime between 1908 and 1918 when the steel bridge was in service. While the street is littered with debris the buildings seem relatively undamaged. (Photographer unknown, collection of Pocahontas County Historical Society)

Jacob Cooper's store in East Cass, with its distinctive three windows on the second floor, changed hands through the years. Later known as Galford's store, it is shown here in use as a West Virginia State Store in the 1970's. Photographed from behind foliage in an empty lot across the road, it gives the impression it was abandoned. (Photo by George A. Fizer)

This small frame building near the junction of "Dirty Street" was used as a liquor store before being run as a grocery in the early 1970's. (Photo by George A. Fizer)

John Reda's Grocery Store at East Cass was at the foot of "Dirty Street". We can only guess if that's John and his family in the photo. (West Virginia and Regional History Collection, West Virginia University Libraries)

The Company Store as operated by the Mower Lumber Company at Cass. The telephone exchange was originally installed in the second floor of the meat market building and continued in service there through the Mower ownership. (Ivan Clarkson Collection, West Virginia State Archives)

Brown Gum, and later Harper Gum, had a store south of Cass near Cold Run and "Slabtown". It seems logical that they served the residents of "Slabtown". The building itself lasted into the late 1970's when it was purchased and dismantled. Evidently the lumber in the structure was more valuable on the open market than the building itself was in Cass. Harper's son, Charlie, went on to run two bars in East Cass. One was across from the location of Max Curry's store, in the building known as Brill's Restaurant. The other was located further east on what is now WV Route 66, but just outside the limits of the incorporated town of Cass.

It doesn't seem possible that either the Reda Store or the Gum Store were serious competition for the Company Store. It truly seems that they were the local convenience stores of the time.

The Mower Lumber Company

When the lumber company, saw mill, and timberlands were sold to Donald and Edwin Mower in 1943 the Company houses and the Pocahontas Supply Company were sold with them. The new owners replaced the store name with their own. The store was identified with a large sign across the front of the building," The Mower Lumber Company". But the goods and services remained essentially the same. It still provided for the needs of the community. In fact a new service was added – dry cleaning of clothing. Special racks were provided to hang the clothes on, which were shipped to Baltimore by train. The cleaned clothes were returned in similar racks and remained on hangers in those racks until claimed by the owners. The extent of the Company Store at Cass was summed up in the headline appearing in the Beckley, West Virginia *Register and Post Herald* on December 17, 1955, "Mammoth General Store at Cass Believed to be Biggest Operated in United States".

The store was also the social center for many of the town residents. They would gather on the front steps in summer and inside the store in winter for the latest gossip and news. Townspeople also congregated in the store at night to listen to the radio located in the furniture department. At train time, the front steps were

The buildings of the Pocahontas Supply Company continued to serve the community after being acquired by the Mower Lumber Company. This February 14, 1947 image shows the overall Company Store, the warehouse to its right and the steel hay storage building beyond. The extent of the canopy above the walkway around the building is also evident. The gas pumps are visible to the left of the C&O locomotive, which is about to leave with a southbound passenger train. (Photo by Ivan O. Clarkson, collection of Roy B. Clarkson)

usually lined with people waiting for the C&O passenger train to arrive so they could look over newly arrived passengers. The regularly scheduled C&O passenger trains were discontinued on January 8, 1958.

At the end of the lumbering operations, in July of 1960, the merchandise in the store was sold at reduced prices. The store continued in business until September 1, 1960 when a "quitting business" sale was held and the entire inventory was sold. Following that sale, the store and its display cases were closed. As a tribute to the Cass residents, the Mower family heirs have noted that when the store was closed virtually all accounts had been settled.

The State Park

The development of the Cass Scenic Railroad by the State of West Virginia brought new life to the old store. The building remained empty until 1963 when

a group of local residents leased it. They operated it as a gift shop where tourists could buy souvenirs, books and clothing. It also provided a small restaurant and an ice cream bar. Managed by Mrs. Jessie Brown Beard Powell, it provided for the needs of the visitors to the state park. The original display cases, the wood floors, and the antiques on display added to the realism of the Company Store setting while complementing the steam locomotives running past the front door. The State of West Virginia purchased the store and its contents in 1976 to be part of the Cass Scenic Railroad State Park. Today it is operated by the State Park as a thriving tourist gift shop. The wood floors creak as visitors walk over them. The display cases glisten with souvenirs, trinkets, and clothing proclaiming "The Cass Scenic Railroad".

The factual history of the Company Store at Cass has been well recorded, but on quiet occasions

The Cass Country Store as operated after acquisition by the State of West Virginia. The previously vacated meat market is used as the post office. (Photographer unknown, courtesy of Cass Scenic Railroad State Park)

the current employees say they can hear someone walking the floors upstairs. They say it's the ghost of one David McDonald; David was the first man to die on the railroad tracks at Cass. He had apparently come to Cass, collected his pay, and wasted it. On his way back to the logging camp he laid down on the tracks for a nap. He probably thought the vibration from an oncoming train would wake him up. It was bad thinking. The next oncoming train didn't wake him and couldn't stop before running him over. His remains were taken to the Company Store until the Coroner arrived. David died on January 30, 1902 and is said to reside today as the "ghost of the store". One can only imagine the tales he might be able to tell us.

Giant icicles hide the second floor windows of the rarely photographed rear of the Company Store at Cass following a significant snow storm. (Photo by Ivan O. Clarkson, collection of Sonny Burruss)

William B. Simmons shown with his dog Tippy; 1917 dog license No. 92, purchased from Company Store and the receipt for that dog license. (Portrait photographer unknown, all items collection of William Sampson)

WOLVERINE

Shoe and Tanning Corporation

Rockford, Michigan

Price List Effective September 10, 1951

••

WOLVERINE SHELL HORSEHIDE WORK SHOES

Style No.	Price	Catalog Page	Style No.	Price	Catalog Page
Solid Brass Nailed			**Goodyear Welt**		
309	$7.60	10	710	$12.35	11
313	7.90	10	711	Discontinued	
507	6.35	10	714	9.90	9
514	6.00	8	717	7.65	7
515	6.00	8	718	7.90	Supplement
517	5.65	8	719	7.10	7
537	5.35	8	721	7.35	7
*537-1	Discontinued		722	7.85	Supplement
*547-1	6.00	Supplement	730	7.60	Supplement
543	5.85	8	736	7.95	9
555	7.75	11	744	7.80	6
588	6.00	8	758	8.15	6
Steel Toe Safety Shoes			762	8.15	6
402	$6.65	12	778	8.65	9
414	7.80	13	*779	7.60	6
604	8.50	12	*789	7.70	Supplement
605	7.45	12	799	8.10	6
606	7.45	12	951	6.70	7
614	8.45	13	964	6.70	7
616	9.30	13	8758	8.80	Supplement
617	7.75	12			
618	7.95	13			
8749	9.80	13			

*537-1 is restyled with seamless backstay as *547-1.
*779 is restyled with seamless backstay as *789.

WOLVERINE ORIGINAL PIGSKIN WORK SHOES

Style No.	Price	Catalog Page	Style No.	Price	Catalog Page
Solid Brass Nail			**Goodyear Welt**		
2613 Boys	$4.35	15	2811 Oxford	$5.35	Supplement
2637	4.85	15	2815 Boys	5.05	Supplement
2639	4.85	Supplement	2838	5.65	15
Steel Toe Safety Shoes			2840	5.90	Supplement
2860	$6.30	Supplement	2844	5.85	15
2864	5.90	Supplement	2878	5.70	Supplement

Prices subject to change without notice. Prices shown are for Sizes 5-11. One pair Size 12 may be included with each dozen pairs at no extra charge. Additional pairs of Size 12 are 25c extra. We do not make Size 11½.

Shoe price list courtesty of Cass Scenic Railroad State Park. Jewelry Department and store bill courtesy of William Sampson.

The Presbyterian Church on Front Street at Cass grew and declined with the fortunes of the lumber industry. Renovated on several occasions, it continues now as the Cass Community Center. (Photo by Sonny Burruss)

Sunday Services
by Gerald M. Futej

The residents of Cass worked hard throughout the week. Sunday, however, was a day of rest and religious worship. Encouraged by WVP&P Co. donations of building materials and sometimes building sites, several Christian denominations had congregations and churches in Cass. All of the churches in Cass were built as wood frame structures.

The oldest of the churches in the town of Cass is the Cass Presbyterian Church. Located prominently next to the Masonic Lodge building at the intersection of Front Street and Luke Street, it was built in 1905. Close examination of vintage town photographs reveals that it has been renovated several times. The original central entrance was relocated when the bell tower was added to the north side. Since then the entrance has been at the base of the bell tower. The wing to the north of the bell tower was added to provide space for congregational meetings and fellowship. Following many years of declining membership the structure was given over and continues to serve the residents today as the Cass Community Center.

Less conspicuous by its location at the intersection of Spruce Street and "A" Street is the Cass United Methodist Church. Built in 1927, it was established as the Methodist Episcopal Church South. Maintained in excellent condition, it is the only active church remaining in Cass.

In East Cass was the Northern Methodist Church. In many ways this building resembled the Presbyterian Church on Front Street. As with the Presbyterian Church, it suffered from declining membership after World War II. In 1951 it was sold to the congregation of the Cass Baptist Church. By the early 1980's, however, it was in poor repair.

Continued disuse allowed it to deteriorate beyond repair. Finally, in 1985 it was razed. Today only an empty space remains.

Close to the bridge on the north side of WV 66 stood another structure used as the Cass Baptist Church. By the 1950's it was no longer used for religious services. It passed through several unsuccessful commercial uses until it was destroyed by the flood of November 5, 1985.

In May of 2005 the fog shrouded mountains to the east contrasted with the apparently bright future enjoyed by the United Methodist Church on Spruce Street at Cass, the only church still in use at Cass today. (Photo by Gerald M. Futej) Above.

The Cass Baptist Church in East Cass as it looked in the mid-1970's. (Photo by George A. Fizer) Right.

The one story frame building just east of the concrete bridge at Cass. Although not always used for religious services it survived until November 5,1985. (Phil Bagdon Collection, West Virginia State Archives) Below.

Very early view of Main Street at Cass, looking north. The edge of the one story frame building at the lower right is believed to be the first school at Cass. Built in 1901 it continued in use until 1908. (Photographer unknown, collection of Pocahontas County Historical Society)

School Days
by Max S. Robin & Gerald M. Futej

Prior to WVP&P Co. coming to Cass the only school in the area was located at Jim McLaughlin's farm, several miles west of the Greenbrier River on a branch of Cold Run. The one room Cold Run School was to the west of the meandering Back Mountain Road, which connected the farms in the area. Two of the teachers at that school were Mr. Frank Hamrick and Mrs. Mamie Hannah.

The school location has been described as "one hollow north of the Cass Cave Hollow". While the school burned down in 1908, Roy Clarkson has noted that its location "was by a grove of Balm of Gilead

trees remaining from a tree planted on the spot prior to 1900".

With the establishment of Cass, the Company initially provided a one story wood frame school on the east side of Main Street near the south end of the Company property. It opened in 1901 with approximately 16 students and Miss Emma Burner as the first teacher. By 1904 Miss Burner was teaching at the Clover Lick School and Mr. Forrest Houchin was teaching at Cass.

The expanding community of Cass quickly outgrew that original building. By 1908 a larger, three room wood frame school was built. Located on the

This undated photo, identified only as "School at Cass", depicts 21 students and apparently two teachers. Believed to be taken at the first school on Main Street, the German siding is similar to that used on the houses at Cass. (Photographer unknown, West Virginia and Regional History Collection, West Virginia University Libraries)

The second school at Cass as seen on August 31, 1963. It was last used as a school in 1915. (Photo by Eugene Burner, collection of Pocahontas County Historical Society)

The Cass Graded School on Main Street, prior to construction of the masonry gymnasium behind the North Wing. (Photographer unknown, collection of Pocahontas County Historical Society)

Taken from nearly the same angle as the photo above, this May 21, 1995 photo clearly shows the masonry gymnasium added in 1949. (Photo by Gerald M. Futej)

hill on the west side of Spruce Street, behind the Superintendent's House, it faced north rather than facing the street. The new school was staffed by Mr. Burley B. Williams, Principal, and Mr. C.F. Hull, Primary Teacher.

The continued growth of the community at Cass soon overtaxed the school on Spruce Street. The establishment of the Range Lumber Company at Deer Creek, south of Cass, in 1910, and the opening of the Extract Plant in 1913 brought additional new families with even more students.

An eight room school was built on the west side of Main Street, south of Cass. This two story wooden frame building with cupola opened in 1915 but apparently was inadequate before it was completed! An architecturally similar four room structure without cupola was added in 1916. The two buildings became known as the South Wing and the North Wing respectively. They housed an enrollment of approximately 400 students under the supervision of Mr. Graham LaRue, the first Principal.

The Burner Annex and the Blackhurst Addition of May 26, 1915, south of the incorporated portion of Cass and east of the Greenbrier River, resulted in almost 100 more 50 foot by 100 foot properties suitable for private residences. The children of those new property owners contributed to the student population. They also encountered a long walk to school. Basically living directly across the river from the school, they had to cross the river on the bridge near the railroad depot in order to get to classes.

Mindful of the problem, the Company provided materials to construct a pedestrian bridge across the river. Extending from East Cass to near the north side of the school building, it consisted of a cable suspended plank floored "swinging bridge" over the river and an elevated walkway across the C&O railroad tracks to the embankment beyond the south end of Front Street. Maintained by the residents of East Cass, the Company provided materials to keep it safe. The bridge lasted until the graded school was closed.

Students and faculty in front of the Cass Graded School. Unfortunately the photo has irreparable damage; however, careful examination allows counting approximately 72 students. Since the school closed in 1970 with an enrollment of 75 students, this may be a photo of the last students to attend the facility on Main Street. (Photographer unknown, courtesy Cass Scenic Railroad State Park)

Students and teachers of the lower grades at the Cass Graded School during lunch. (Photographer unknown, courtesy Cass Scenic Railroad State Park)

Student servers; Tammy Crist, Veronica Swink, and Kim Hickson (l to r) and adult moderators; Opal Arborgat, Nina Brooks, and Melba Hickson, ready for the "lunch rush" at the Cass Graded School. (Photographer unknown, courtesy Cass Scenic Railroad State Park)

J. K. Arbogast
Principal
Sci. & Civ.

Vera Swadley
Math. & Music

Glen Tracy
Soc. Studies
English

Ruby Gum
Grades 5 & 6

Wilmer Ruckman
Grades 4 & 5

Louise Brown
Grade 3

Lynn Kerr
Grade 2

Ruth Riley
Grade 1

Faculty of the Cass school. ca 1960. (Photographer unknown, courtesy of Cass Scenic Railroad State Park)

A view of the south side of the Cass Graded School shows the four classroom portion behind the South Wing. (Photo by Ivan O. Clarkson, collection of Sonny Burruss)

Situated on Main Street south of the incorporated town limits, the Cass Graded School was affected by the increasing use of automobiles. Just like much larger towns, the need for school crossing guards in Cass soon became apparent. Eighth grade boys were provided with badges and safety patrol belts. Assigned to specific intersections along Main Street, they were tasked with safely escorting their younger schoolmates across the street.

The Cass Graded School consisted of grades one through nine. During the 1920's a Junior High Department was established. The Junior High students used the first floor, while Primary students were taught on the second floor. The arrangement continued through 1931 when Mr. Mack Brooks was Principal with 10 teachers and 330 students. In 1932 the Junior High Department closed and the students were bused to the Green Bank High School.

A masonry block gymnasium was added behind the North Wing in 1949. Reportedly the largest school gymnasium in Pocahontas County, it was used by the county high school basketball teams on many occasions.

In keeping with the custom of the times, a separate school was provided for black students. The one room school was held in the Baptist Church, near the bridge, in East Cass. Over the years Hattie Holley, Sydney and Marie Goodwin, and Ida Choice taught there. It served those students from 1917 until 1956 when they were admitted to the Cass Graded School.

Ted Shinaberry, member of the safety patrol, posed for his school photo in 1940. (Photographer unknown, collection of Ted Shinaberry)

Ernestine Clarkson on the swinging bridge over the Greenbrier River leading to East Cass. (Photo by Ivan O. Clarkson, collection of Sonny Burruss)

The snow covered walkway from the swinging bridge leading to the west side of the Greenbrier River. The Cass Graded School is at left in the background. Left. (Photo by Ivan O. Clarkson, collection of Sonny Burruss)

Following the boom years of the logging industry, the local population declined to about the pre-1900 levels. As a result, by 1970 the enrollment at the Cass Graded School declined to 75 students and five teachers. At that time the Cass school was consolidated with the Green Bank Graded School.

Since then, time and the environment have gradually reclaimed the buildings. A lack of maintenance, or justification for its continued use, has resulted in the collapse and demolition of the South Wing. One can only speculate on how long the North Wing will survive.

THE CASS BUGLE

Vol. 1   April 8, 1938

THE MARBLE TOURNAMENT

Marble season is here again, nearly all the boys seem to be excited over the fact that the marble tournament is soon to be held. The tournament will begin by singling out the best player from each grade. These boys will compete in numerous games until the champion is found. The winner of the school contest will enter the county tournament at Marlinton. The one who wins in the county will be eligible for the state tournament at Clarksburg. The state champion will be given a free trip to Atlantic City. Boys, shine up your marbles as we can boast of a champion.

Jokes

Grandmother: Johnny, when I was little like you, I knew all the historical men and sites.
Johnny: Yes, but there weren't so many then.

Geno: Which is correct to say Bill or William?
Billy: William is correct.
Geno: Well, then I suppose that chicken has a William.

Jack: This liniment makes my arm smart.
Bob: Why don't you rubsome of it on your head?

THE WORLD

The world is in an uproar
With war on every hand;
Battles raging wildly
And unrest in every land.
Hitler seized Austria
And now is in command,
While China keeps on fighting
With her enemy, Japan.
The U. S. remains neutral
Which puts her on the spot,
For allthe disputes and arguments
Are bound to become hot
The land of Czechoslovakia
Is being backed by France
So when Hilter starts to meddle
He is taking a big chance.
Here's hoping that all nations
Can find some terms of peace,
So that all the bitter war
And dread fighting soon will cease.

Cover and excerpts from the April 1938 issue of the Cass Graded School newspaper. (courtesy of Cass Scenic Railroad State Park) Eighth grade class ring property of Barbara Simmons Sampson. (Photo by William Sampson)

The Pocahontas Supply Company provided space and the Postmaster to run the U.S. Post Office at Cass, West Virginia. The sign over the door of this 1910 vintage photo proclaims its location. (Photographer unknown, collection of Richard Dale)

Neither Snow, Nor Rain...
by Gerald M. Futej

Soon after the decision to develop the town of Cass at Leatherbark Ford, it became necessary to provide postal service. A portion of the original Pocahontas Supply Company store was designated as the U.S. Post Office. Initially employees of West Virginia Pulp & Paper Company were also designated as the Postmaster at Cass.

Throughout the renovations and expansions of the Company Store, the postal facilities were included in the floor plan. However, when the store closed in 1960 the post office was housed in the former Nethken Meat Market building.

In the early 1980's the Postal Service provided a large mobile home-type trailer to house the Post Office at Cass. Located on the east side of WV Route 66, at its junction with "Dirty Street" in East Cass, this trailer served well until the flood of 1985. The raging waters of the Greenbrier River engulfed the trailer and

destroyed its contents. Surprisingly, the trailer remained in place, but it was no longer usable.

Maude Moore was Postmaster from July 1984 until May 1996. She recalls that after the trailer was damaged by the flood she would take the mail to the depot in her car. There she would "hand" deliver the mail to the residents who came to pick it up.

Ultimately the trailer was removed. The Cass Post Office was reestablished in the former meat market adjacent to the Company Store. It has remained there since then.

Thanks to the thoughtfulness of Maude Moore and her successors, we have the list of the Postmasters that served the Post Office at Cass, West Virginia 24927.

Cass Post Office
Pocahontas County, West Virginia
24927

POSTMASTERS	TITLE	APPOINTED
Jasper S. Mathews	Postmaster	02/25/1901
Zackwell M. Ayers	Postmaster	04/14/1915
Robert S. Hickman	Acting Postmaster	07/01/1919
Samuel L. Clark	Postmaster	07/27/1920
Ray W. Fox	Acting Postmaster	02/03/1933
James H. Moyer	Acting Postmaster	04/01/1933
James H. Moyer	Postmaster	02/28/1934
Frank C. Nickell	Acting Postmaster	04/16/1945
Frank C. Nickell	Postmaster	07/17/1947
Mrs. Evelyn D. Lightner	Acting Postmaster	04/30/1960
Mrs. Evelyn D. Lightner	Postmaster	10/08/1962
Kermit Friel	Officer-in-Charge	03/29/1984
Mrs. Maude S. Moore	Postmaster	07/21/1984
Nanette Beckurth	Officer-in-Charge	05/03/1996
Jim Bibey	Postmaster	09/30/1996
Bernice Taylor	Postmaster	07/30/1998
Vicki J. Schaffner	Officer-in-Charge	02/02/2001
Nanette Beckurth	Postmaster	08/11/2001
Bernard G. King	Officer-in-Charge	09/10/2002
Jennifer L. Hefner	Officer-in-Charge	01/08/2003
Bernard G. King	Postmaster	08/09/2003
Mrs. Linda D. Elza	Officer-in-Charge	08/25/2006
Ancil E. Parks	Postmaster	02/16/2007

After the Mower Lumber Company sold the Company Store the Post Office was housed in the former Nethken Meat Market building. Except for a short period when a mobile trailer, located in East Cass, was used the Post Office has been at this location. (Photo by Barbara B. Futej)

The short-lived Post Office in a trailer which was damaged during the flood of 1985 and removed. (Photo by Sonny Burruss)

The Ford Roadster parked on Main Street on May 20, 2005 was reminiscent of the mid-1930's at Cass. (Photo by Gerald M. Futej)

I Remember Cass
compiled by Gerald M. Futej

The following comments provide some insight into living, working, or growing up in Cass. Written from notes taken during discussions at Cass or letters written by former residents, they provide small slices of life in and around the Company Town. I hope you enjoy the memories.

Guy "Bones" Stanley was my father. He was a railroad engineer for the Western Maryland Railway and worked the trains from Spruce. He would take the lumber company train from Cass to Spruce.

In 1942 he transferred to another job at Vindex, WV. It was still the Western Maryland Railway there. He told Mom the houses there were "pretty nice". So we packed all our things in boxes and put them in a truck. All the children rode in the back of the truck with the boxes.

We left Cass in the evening. It took us all night to get from Cass to Vindex. When we got there Mother was so mad at him. That house didn't even have water! Not even a well!! We had to carry water to the house in buckets.

I think one reason Dad wanted to work there was because the Western Maryland had a Shay locomotive there. It was the Chaffee branch, you know, with a coal mine at the top. Well, one day Dad and his fireman wanted to finish early so they could go hunting. They were coming down the hill a bit too fast. They lost control and wrecked that train. There was coal all over the place! The railroad took the engine to Ridgley to be fixed. Good thing he didn't do that with the new engine, Western Maryland Shay No. 6, otherwise it might not be here at Cass now.

- Pearl Stanley (Nasti)

Mom worked at Kane's store for almost 40 years. She and Dad used to run the Company Store at

Slaty Fork. When it closed they moved back to Cass, then got a house in East Cass. Dad worked at the millpond. She was a clerk and bookkeeper at Kane's Store. She worked until the store closed for the day, then Dad and I would drive over to pick her up and go home.

I would run over to grandma's behind the store, it was by Jim White's, for lunch and then go back to school. There was a warehouse next to the store. They used to clean wool there. It was always dusty. For a while they showed movies in that warehouse, later on they used the auditorium in the school to show movies.
- *Gary McPherson*

As long as I can remember the houses at Cass were painted white. Even on the old photos all the houses seem to be the same tone. On some photos the depot looks much darker, like its not white, or light gray. But when we used the houses at Cass we painted the window trim light green. Green and white were the colors of the racing silks for Aunt Dorothy's race horses from PocaDot Farm.
- *D. Roger Mower*

My wife, Verna, and I visited Rupert, WV one time. She saw the street signs there and suggested they would be good at Cass. When we got back to Cass I ordered the signs we have now.
- *Richard Dale*

Cass could be a pretty rough place. Especially when the wood hicks were here. The kids were not allowed to go to East Cass when the wood hicks were there. There was a lot of drinking and fights then.
- *Pearl Stanley (Nasti)*

Everett and I first went housekeeping over the Brown Gum store after he came home from service. In May of 1946 we moved into the house next to Kane's Store and Everett worked in the Planner Mill. Rent was only $12.00 per month., but the wages were low. The Company gave wallpaper and paint when it was needed but the renter had to do the work. We had good neighbors and they helped one another if needed. After the mill closed Everett went to work for National Radio Astronomy Observatory.
- *Betty Jane Arbogast*

Kane's Store, to the right, and the Company House, at left, look about the same on May 20, 2005 as they did when Everett and Betty Jane Arborgast lived there in 1946. (Photo by Gerald M. Futej)

The C&O gas electric "Doodle Bug" waited to board passengers like Maude Moore, at the Cass depot before continuing south to Stony Bottom and beyond. (Photo by Ivan O. Clarkson, collection of Sonny Burruss)

When we first moved to Stony Bottom, I didn't have a car. When I needed to go shopping I would "flag" the C&O train at Stony Bottom and ride up to Cass. I could do my shopping in the Company Store. The train would go all the way to Durbin, and then come back. I'd get back on at the depot at Cass and then ride back to Stony Bottom.

- *Maude Moore*

We had a cow named "Cherry". The cows were allowed to graze in the pasture up north of the Club House. But every night we had to drive the cow home. Kept it in a barn behind the house on Front Street. We'd drive it right down Main Street, leaving cow manure all along the way.

- *Gary McPherson*

I'm a city girl, you know. My husband, Bill, and I moved here from Charleston, WV in 1950. We moved to Bill's grandmother's home at Stony Bottom. To get there we drove right down Main Street. The first time I saw Cass it was so beautiful. Each house had a white picket fence and colorful flowers. It looked like a Hollywood movie set to me.

- *Maude Moore*

I grew up in Mace, WV, which is on Route 219, a bit north of the lodge at Snowshoe. It's maybe 10 or 12 miles from Cass. My grandfather worked on a section gang for the railroad. That was the railroad built by WVP&P Co., which they later sold to the Western Maryland Railway and eventually became part of the CSX.

Both Grandpa and Grandma had a big influence on me. Grandpa told me stories about working on the railroad. Grandma forbade me going to Cass. "It's just too dangerous", she would say. I listened to her, but I always wondered what was on the other side of Cheat Mountain.

When Grandma passed away, I waited two years before I ventured to Cass. I drove over the mountain road and fell in love with the little town. That was in 1985. Now I work in the depot at the Scenic Railroad and meet visitors from all over the world. Somehow Cass isn't so dangerous as Grandma told me. But I'm sure it was different when she was my age.

- *Tammy Shoemaker*

My first job was working on the Mower farm along Deer Creek. It was summer and they were takin' in hay. The hay was baled and had to be hoisted up to the hay loft in the barn. They had a rope went over some pulleys and was hitched to some mules. I gave the mule driver the signal when to pull that rope and when to stop.

When they asked me if I wanted a job I said "Yes!" Nowadays if you ask someone if they want a job they say "How much does it pay?" Boy, times sure have changed!!

- Artie Barkley

East Cass could be a pretty exciting place to live. On Saturday night we would go to the "Saturday Night Fights". There were plenty of places to drink up by the bridge. Sooner or later there would be a fight. They usually started inside a bar but fell out into the street. We just waited around on the boardwalk until a fight started. It was the best entertainment in town!

- Thurmond Sampson

My grandfather was a wood hick. He worked on the mountain cutting timber for the mill and only got home once a month. When grandmother died my Mom had to take care of her brothers Arthur, Stanley, and Brooks White.

My Dad ran away and joined the Navy. He got TB and was sent home to Cass. He couldn't work so he kept the house and Mom worked at the Mower Lumber Company Store.

I think back to how times have changed so much, my Dad being disabled spent a lot of time with the retired men in town as he had a lot of time on his hands. One of the places he hung out was Onney Plyers store with a couple of gas pumps outside. I used to just go behind the counter and get myself some candy always thinking Mr. Onney was such a nice man to let me have that candy, not knowing until later in life that he was counting what I got and my Dad paid for it. One day I went back there and came out with a pistol, I said "Stick it up, Mr. Onney" he said "Joe, can't you see I'm talking". Again I said "Stick it up!", it was then that my Dad realized that it was a real pistol that Onney had forgot was there, and it was loaded. Needless to say, he was much more careful about that pistol from then on.

- Joe Jackson

By the time I got to Junior High School we were bused to the school at Green Bank. We were a "consolidated" school district before consolidation was invented.

Teenagers gather at Kirkpatrick's Restaurant in East Cass. In the background is the Alpha Hotel, a wood hick's stop when in town. (Photographer unknown, courtesy Cass Scenic Railroad State Park)

The Mayor's Office and Council Chambers on Luke Street at Cass were built above the four cell brick walled jail. The large iron door led to the jail cells. (Photo by Sonny Burruss)

We had six classes a day, four subjects, physical education and a free period for study or sports practice. But our education was pretty good. From the houses on Front Street alone there was Bill Irvin, became a doctor. Mavin Dill, son of a sawyer at the mill became a dentist. So did Jim Williams, son of Piney Williams the locomotive engineer.

- Gary McPherson

Joe Woodall was the only cop I remember that shot somebody dead in Cass. Apparently it was a pretty busy night for Joe. He had all four cells in the jail full, so he put one guy in the "bullpen" between the cells. Well that guy tore the stovepipe off the stove and came at Joe yelling "I'll kill you!"

Joe shot him first, and then investigated to see what happened. Joe was the last cop in Cass.

- Gary McPherson

You know Lefty Meeks, the barber? He's been cutting hair here for about 45 years. When I was a kid the barber was Butch Wilma. He gave me my first haircut on a box at my grandfather's house, behind Kane's store.

Then there was Bourbor Nicely, he was the town barber that suffered from palsy. He always hollared at you to "HOLD STILL!"

- Gary McPherson

I was born in 1936 in a house on Front Street. Doctor Hannah delivered me. So I was in first grade when we got into World War II. The whole community supported the war effort. The adults had scrap drives collecting paper and tin and aluminum. On Fridays at school the kids would help. We pealed the aluminum foil off gum wrappers, or took the wool out of milkweed pods, they told us it was for insulation in flight jackets for pilots. I don't know if that was really true, but when I was six years old I was convinced I was helping to win the war.

- *Gary McPherson*

The stories about the wood hicks on "Dirty Street" are true. They would come into town on the log train. They'd jump off and head right for the bridge to East Cass. You could see sparks fly from the nails on the caulked boots as they ran across that concrete.

After a while there would usually be a fight. Lots of times they would march out of town, down Main Street to fight. That way they would be out of the town limits and not subject to the town cop. As they went down Main Street the crowd of spectators following would get bigger. I liked to hang around to see what would happen. Sometimes when Joe Woodall, the cop, had trouble handling a problem he would just deputize the people around and they would have to help him.

My folks used that as a threat. They'd say "If you go up there Joe Woodall will make you a deputy." That threat worked ... for a while.

- *Gary McPherson*

My dad was a locomotive engineer so we moved around quite a bit. I was born in Spruce but lived in and around Cass from 1926 to 1942. During the 1930's we lived at Deer Creek.

In the summer the school children all had chores to do at home. After those were done we could see our friends. I knew the Slaven girls. Somehow they had a way to get scripts for plays, like theatre plays. They would practice the parts and then have a performance. They lived up on Spruce Street where it was pretty hilly, so one end of the house was high off the ground. They used the space under the house for the theatre. We all paid admission to go see the plays. A hair pin or a safety pin was enough to get in.

- *Pearl Stanley (Nasti)*

Our family has been in Cass for quite some time. My grandfather Lambert was a logger. He worked on the mountain for Mower Lumber. My grandfather Neighbors worked at the saw mill, he blew the whistle at noon.

I grew up in East Cass, the Blackhurst Addition. Mom and Dad had their house there. Like the other

The interior of the jail is pretty sparce with only a commode and three iron cots hinged to the wall of each cell. A potbelly stove is there but probably didn't heat the brick walls very well. (Photo by Sonny Burruss)

69

kids there we walked the swinging bridge to and from school.

I think the kids were pretty sheltered then. We didn't hear much about the wood hicks, or "Dirty Street". Downtown Cass, by the bridge, was off limits but at school we had a half hour for lunch and we would go to the Company Store for ice cream. It was only a nickel.

- *Mary Neighbors (Snyder)*

Mom and Dad moved to Baltimore when the mill closed in 1960. It was sad because both their grandfathers moved to Cass to get jobs. Anyway, we still have relatives that live in, or near, Cass and we visit them frequently.

One year Mom and Dad went to Aunt Bertie's for Thanksgiving and my brother and I left Baltimore after work to join them. By the time we got to Front Royal it started snowing and when we got to the crest of Alleghany Mountain there was 3 or 4 inches on the road.

Now I don't know where the snow plow was. They must have been saving it for the parade, because we never saw it all the way to Cass.

- *Bill Sampson*

I was a planer operator for 20 years at the mill. We ran special machines to make flooring and wooden molding for houses.

I was married just 6 weeks when I got drafted for the war (World War II), went to the Army, and I didn't get back for three years. When I got back the Mowers owned the mill. They gave us the lumber and I helped the tenants build the picket fences in 1946 or 47.

Back then house rent was $10.50 a month up on the hill, $12.50 a month on Front Street. My wife, Jeanette, and I liked it on Front Street. I have been living in that same house for 53 years.

- *Jim White*

This snow scene on Main Street at Cass in the late 1950's is a reminder of the cold winters that many people have spent there over the years. (Photo by Ivan O. Clarkson, collection of Sonny Burruss)

Mrs. Mary Urbanic and her boys (l to r) Joe, Rudy, and Albine in their "Sunday Best" on Bohunk Hill at Cass. (Photographer unknown, Vlademir Maleckar Collection, West Virginia State Archives)

My Daddy, Louis Savich, came from Austria to work in a logging camp on the mountain. He married my mother, Stella, and moved to Cass to work in the shop. They lived on Bohunk Hill from 1926 until 1948, when he passed away. My brother, Eddie, and I grew up there.

Our neighbors were Joe and Mary Urbanic. Mr. Urbanic worked in the mill. Later he became foreman and they moved to the Company house. They had three sons; Joe, Albine, and Rudy. Rudy eventually became a teacher.

The Tdershoes lived on Bohunk Hill too. They had seven children; John, Adam, Sam, Columbia, Colmia, Catherine, and Ruthie. My best friends were Nan and Tenie Myers. We were like one big family. We played games like I Spy, Kick the Can, and marbles. We would walk down the path to the Company Store to see the mail train come in and maybe some people. If I had a couple of pennies, my bright light of the day was going in the Company Store, standing on my tip toes, and putting my pennies on the counter to get gum balls.

When I went to school my first grade teacher was Mrs. Thurman and the principal was Mr. Arborgast. At Greenback High School, Mr.Blackhurst was my teacher.

In the summer, after the mill whistle blew at 12:00 for the mill to start up, I would wash the dishes and get ready to go swimming with my girfriends Marie Irvin and Louelle. For fun we went to Kirkpatrick's Restaurant to dance on Saturday nights or to the schoolhouse to see movies.

All just great memories.
- *Mary Ethel Savich (Day)*

Tom Myles posed with the water tank from Shay No. 8 (c/n 2583) on May 20, 1989, at Old Spruce on the Cass Scenic Railroad. The 1912 product of Lima Locomotive Works was lettered G.C.& E., for the Greenbrier, Cheat, and Elk Railroad. Tom's grandfather, Alfred Harvey Myles, was the conductor assigned to No. 8 when he worked at Cass prior to 1917. (Photo by Gerald M. Futej)

A Cass Connection
by Gerald M. Futej

Job opportunities create great changes in our lives. When I had the opportunity to move my family closer to our immediate relatives, both my wife and I jumped at the chance. We moved from North Carolina to Southeastern Pennsylvania in 1976. While I was busy with my new job, my wife became involved with the elementary school that our children attended. It was a great way for her to meet new people and become familiar with the area.

Within a few months she met Carmen, another school volunteer mother who was also a newcomer. I soon met Carmen's husband, Tom. He was a career railroader, which Carmen acknowledged had stressfully resulted in living in 19 different places in a span of only 20 years. As Tom and I spoke, I told him of a planned trip to Railfan Weekend at the Cass Scenic Railroad. "Is that Cass, West Virginia?" Tom inquired. "I have relatives that lived there," he said excitedly. Well that was it, the ladies never heard from us the rest of the night!

Tom is also an amateur genealogist, and focuses on the Myles family. With the advent of the personal computer and scanner technology, Tom now has reams of family information at his finger tips. While his records go back much further, my interest in them goes back only to the 1890's.

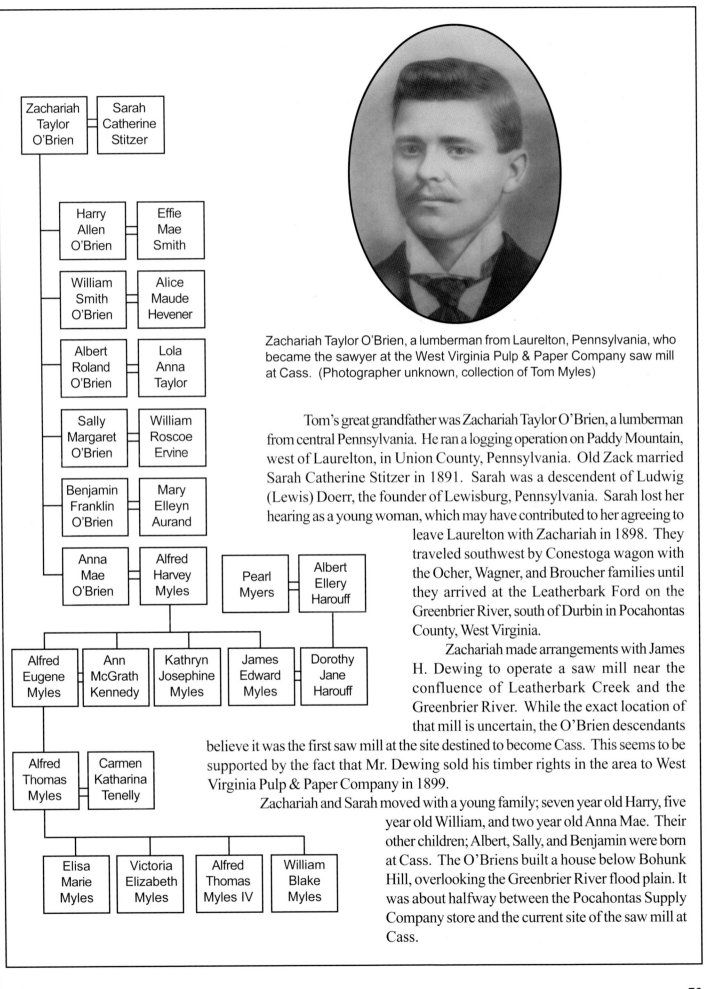

Zachariah Taylor O'Brien, a lumberman from Laurelton, Pennsylvania, who became the sawyer at the West Virginia Pulp & Paper Company saw mill at Cass. (Photographer unknown, collection of Tom Myles)

Tom's great grandfather was Zachariah Taylor O'Brien, a lumberman from central Pennsylvania. He ran a logging operation on Paddy Mountain, west of Laurelton, in Union County, Pennsylvania. Old Zack married Sarah Catherine Stitzer in 1891. Sarah was a descendent of Ludwig (Lewis) Doerr, the founder of Lewisburg, Pennsylvania. Sarah lost her hearing as a young woman, which may have contributed to her agreeing to leave Laurelton with Zachariah in 1898. They traveled southwest by Conestoga wagon with the Ocher, Wagner, and Broucher families until they arrived at the Leatherbark Ford on the Greenbrier River, south of Durbin in Pocahontas County, West Virginia.

Zachariah made arrangements with James H. Dewing to operate a saw mill near the confluence of Leatherbark Creek and the Greenbrier River. While the exact location of that mill is uncertain, the O'Brien descendants believe it was the first saw mill at the site destined to become Cass. This seems to be supported by the fact that Mr. Dewing sold his timber rights in the area to West Virginia Pulp & Paper Company in 1899.

Zachariah and Sarah moved with a young family; seven year old Harry, five year old William, and two year old Anna Mae. Their other children; Albert, Sally, and Benjamin were born at Cass. The O'Briens built a house below Bohunk Hill, overlooking the Greenbrier River flood plain. It was about halfway between the Pocahontas Supply Company store and the current site of the saw mill at Cass.

The O'Brien children at Cass, (l to r) Albert Roland, Harry Allen, Anna Mae, Sally Margaret, and William Smith, ca 1903. (Photo by E.F. Jones, Ronceverte, West Virginia, collection of Tom Myles)

Sarah Catherine Stitzer O'Brien with her youngest son, Benjamin Franklin O'Brien, on the boardwalk in front of the O'Brien house at Cass, ca 1908. (Photographer unknown, collection of Tom Myles)

Apparently, Zachariah was hired by E.P. Schaffer when the Luke family and Joseph Cass purchased the timber rights from James Dewing and set up the West Virginia Pulp and Paper Company saw mill at the mouth of Leatherbark Creek. Zachariah was a sawyer at the Cass saw mill. He supervised and directed the actual timber sawing operation inside the mill. His nearby house was very convenient to his work site at the mill. But that convenience may have contributed to his untimely death on September 21, 1906, at age 32. According to his obituary in the Lewisburg, Pennsylvania newspaper, he was returning home from the mill at night when he was struck by a train about two hundred feet from his house. It was reported that he was taken to a nearby hospital where he died three hours later, with his wife and six children in attendance. At that time, the closest hospital would have been adjacent to Dr. Randolph's house, in Cass; transport to any other location within three hours would have been improbable.

Sarah raised their children; Harry, William, Anna Mae, Albert, Sally, and Benjamin at the O'Brien house in Cass. The O'Brien descendants have long held that she supported the youngsters by baking bread and selling it in town. However, I have not been able to confirm that with any longtime Cass residents.

Eventually, Harry moved to Ohio and raised a family. William married Alice Maude Hevener, who raised their family at Cass while he was employed in Winchester, Virginia. Sally married William Roscoe Ervine and stayed in Cass. Benjamin went to Brownsville, Pennsylvania to work on the railroad. There he met and married Mary Ellen Aurand.

In a strange twist of fate, Zachariah O'Brien's son, Albert Roland O'Brien also died on the Greenbrier Subdivision of the C&O Railroad. He was injured when attempting to get off a moving north bound freight train at Durbin, and died on August 13, 1929. His daughter, Bertina, later married Thurmond Cosner. They lived in the last house next to WV Route 66 as you drive toward Route 28 from East Cass.

Tom's grandmother, Anna Mae O'Brien was courted by Albert "Sam" Harouff, formerly of Edray, West Virginia. At about the same time, Alfred Harvey Myles of Renick, West Virginia moved to the hotel at Cass. He worked as a conductor on the logging railroad, assigned to Shay locomotive No. 8. Family legend has it that one morning as No. 8 passed the O'Brien house, Anna Mae was on the porch. Alfred exclaimed, "That's the girl I'm going to marry!" and eventually he did.

Sam Harouff and Alfred Myles were good friends, as were Anna Mae O'Brien and Pearl Myers. At sometime the relationship between Sam and Anna Mae cooled and Alfred stepped in. At the time, courting at Cass included picnics and Sunday afternoon walks around the town and the saw mill. Alfred and Anna Mae were married at Marlinton in 1917. Later, Sam married Pearl and stayed at Cass.

Alfred Harvey Myles and Anna Mae soon moved to Brownsville, Pennsylvania when he took a job as a conductor on the Pennsylvania Railroad. They eventually raised three children, Alfred Eugene, Kathryn Josephine, and James Edward.

Alfred Eugene Myles married Ann McGrath Therese Kennedy in 1942. Alfred Eugene followed in his father's footsteps as a career railroader, eventually rising to Vice President and Director of Engineering on the Chicago and Northwestern Railroad. My friend Tom was born in 1944 and was christened Alfred Thomas

Albert Roland O'Brien with his children Robert Eugene O'Brien (l) and Bertina Elizabeth O'Brien (r), at Cass, ca 1923. (Photographer unknown, collection of Tom Myles)

Anna Mae O'Brien and Albert Ellery "Sam" Harouff. Apparently someone "removed" Sam from a similar photo. Perhaps Anna Mae gave the "cropped" photo to her new beau, Alfred Harvey Myles. (Photographer unknown, both photos collection of Tom Myles)

Sam Harouff (l) and Alfred Harvey Myles in a state of the art runabout at Cass. The steps to the left and boardwalk behind the car suggest this was taken on Front Street near the hotel that they lived in at Cass, ca 1915. (Photographer unknown, collection of Tom Myles) Above.

Anna Mae O'Brien and her good friend Pearl Myers posed in their "Sunday Best" on the porch swing at the O'Brien house in Cass, ca 1915. (Photographer unknown, collection of Tom Myles) Right.

Alfred Harvey Myles and Anna Mae O'Brien posed separately on the footboard of Shay locomotive No. 8 (c/n 2583) at Cass during the traditional "Sunday Afternoon Walk". Alfred was assigned to No. 8 as conductor, ca 1916. (Photographer unknown, collection of Tom Myles)

Zachariah O'Brien's house at Cass (r) was maintained by his wife who raised their six children there. The other house was used by the Brice family. Mr. Brice was the C&O station agent. (Photographer unknown, collection of Tom Myles)

Anna Mae and Alfred Myles with a car full of friends on an outing near Cass, West Virginia. While Anna Mae was behind the wheel, she never learned to drive a car!!, ca 1917. (Photographer unknown, collection of Tom Myles)

Myles. In keeping with the "Alfred Myles" tradition, Tom also became a railroader. A retired Conrail employee, he now operates his own railcar cleaning and repair service, assisted by his sons Tom and Bill.

He remembers attending his Uncle James' wedding in Cass in 1949. Interestingly, his uncle, James Edward Myles, married Dorothy Harouff, the daughter of Sam Harouff and Pearl Myers! The ceremony was performed by Reverend Blackhurst. An intimate family gathering followed at the Blackhurst residence in East Cass. Tom has no other recollection of visiting Cass as a youngster.

After several years of persuasion, I finally got Tom to return to Cass in May of 1989 with his wife Carmen and their sons Tom and Bill. Perhaps their daughters, Elisa and Vicky, weren't as interested as the boys were in seeing steam engines or braving the cloudy damp weather on Cheat Mountain that day.

The Myles family at Blainsburg, PA, (l to r) Alfred Eugene Myles, Anna Mae O'Brien Myles and Alfred Harvey Myles, ca 1919. (Photographer unknown, collection of Tom Myles)

Uncle James' wedding at the Blackhurst home in East Cass, July 1949 (l to r) "Icey", Alfred Eugene Myles, Donald Harouff, Pearl Myers Harouff, Donald Harouff's guest, Sam Harouff, Anna Mae O'Brien Myles, James Edward Myles, Alfred Harvey Myles, Jane Harouff Myles. (Photographer unknown, collection of Tom Myles)

Sam Harouff (r) and unknown trainman (l) posed on the footboard of Shay No. 5 (c/n 1503) at the Cass locomotive shop. The wood cab and kerosene headlamp on the locomotive suggest that the photo was taken prior to 1921. (Photographer unknown, collection of Tom Myles)

Tom's visits to Cass have been few and far between. But when you talk with him it becomes obvious that he is proud of everything his relatives have accomplished and he cherishes his family's connection to Cass.

Almost 70 years after Sam Harouff posed in the photo above, Tom and Carmen Myles posed with their sons Bill and Tom in front of Shay No. 5, at the Cass Scenic Railroad, May 20, 1989. (Photo by Gerald M. Futej)

Class Three House No. 133 on Front Street, the only street at Cass with concrete sidewalks, is representative of the Company Houses built by West Virginia Pulp & Paper Company. Even the front porch railing and vertical skirting below it match those seen in early photos of Cass. (Photo by Sonny Burruss)

The Houses at Cass

by Max S. Robin

The most numerous of the Company Houses at Cass have been identified as "Class Three Houses". Built as rental properties, they were owned by West Virginia Pulp & Paper Company. They were rented to Company day laborers with families.

Built to a standardized floor plan, they served as a basis for the design of the Class Two Houses and many of the Class One Houses. Early photos of Cass, ca 1902, show twenty-four houses of which five appear to be still under construction. By the mid-1920's as many as 50 Class Three Houses can be identified. While many of these were transferred to the Mower

Lumber Company in 1942, several were sold to private owners after the Mower Lumber operations closed in 1960.

Currently there are about 40 structures at Cass that were originally built as Class Three Houses. Several of those are still privately owned and many have been modified. Of the 33 Class Three Houses owned by the State of West Virginia, 19 are available for rental by visitors to the Cass Scenic Railroad State Park. There are presently 14 houses which are not available for rental, many of which are badly deteriorated and may not be able to be restored.

The application for inclusion on the National Register of Historic Places (NRHP) describes the Class Three Houses architecturally as:

"Houses built in Cass by the company for its "day-laborers" are very stout, rectangular, two-story, six-room frames with front and rear porches. They have fronts of two-bays and foundations of large timbers on blocks. Gable ends are front and rear, and the roof slope is medium. Porches are one-story, eight feet deep, and they have shed-roofs. Every company-owned building in Cass, except one, was, and is now, weatherboarded with "German" siding (a narrow beveled type introduced in the early 1900's). These thirty by twenty foot houses have central chimneys to serve wood or coal burning stoves in any or all rooms. The foundations are covered by vertical boards or they are hidden behind lattice work, and on this sloping land this provides a protected storage space. Roofs are now covered with roll roofing and perhaps always have been so covered. Windows are plain, 2/2 double-hung sash. On the stairway side of the house the windows are not evenly placed, but on the opposite side most houses have two-bays or five windows.

All class three houses have interior plans as standardized as are the exteriors. The entrance door opens into a hall which contains a single-flight stairway. To the left of the hall is a 17 by 17 foot (sic) living room, and behind it is a 13 by 12 foot (sic) dining room. Ceilings are eight feet high, wall coverings are plaster with plain trim. There is nothing ornamental about these houses, inside or out. On the rear porch is a pantry with a door from the kitchen. An upstairs hall gives access to three bedrooms. Sometime, about 1918 according to some persons, bathrooms were built in the front of the upstairs hall. Originally, every one of these houses had a white picket fence which enclosed their yards which were dotted with old-time flowers. At the rear of each lot, on the alley, a small storage building was built for a supply of wood and coal. In later times, small garages were built here and along each side of each street were board walks."

In the mid 1980's, House #320 was considered the ideal example of a Class Three House.

Looking down the backyards on the west side of Main Street, the window placement and the rear porch enclosures on the Class Three Houses are readily apparent. (Photo by Barbara B. Futej)

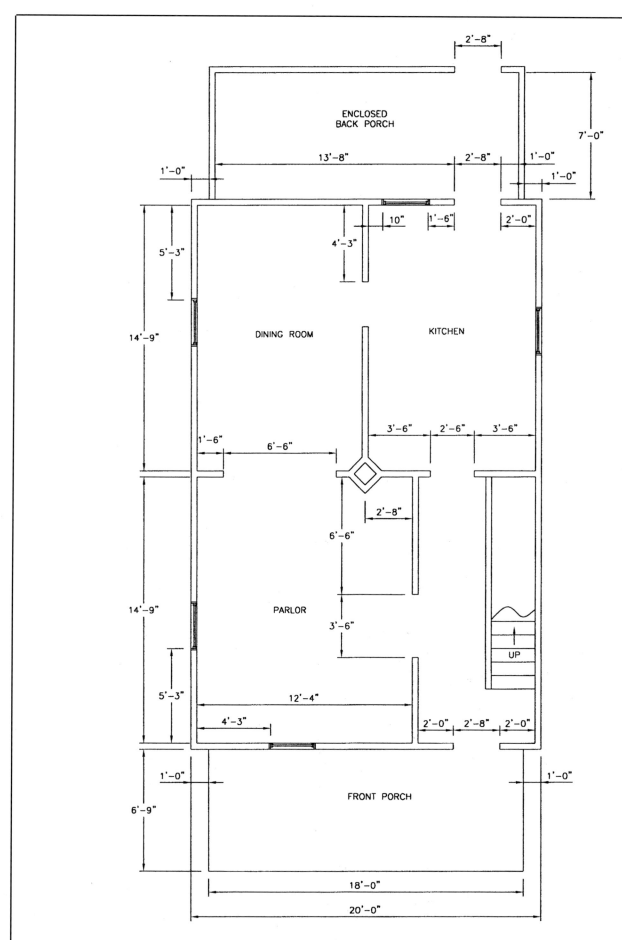

Interior arrangement of the first floor of Class Three House No. 332 on Spruce Street. (Drawn from measurements taken by Max S. Robin and Gerald M. Futej in May 1993)

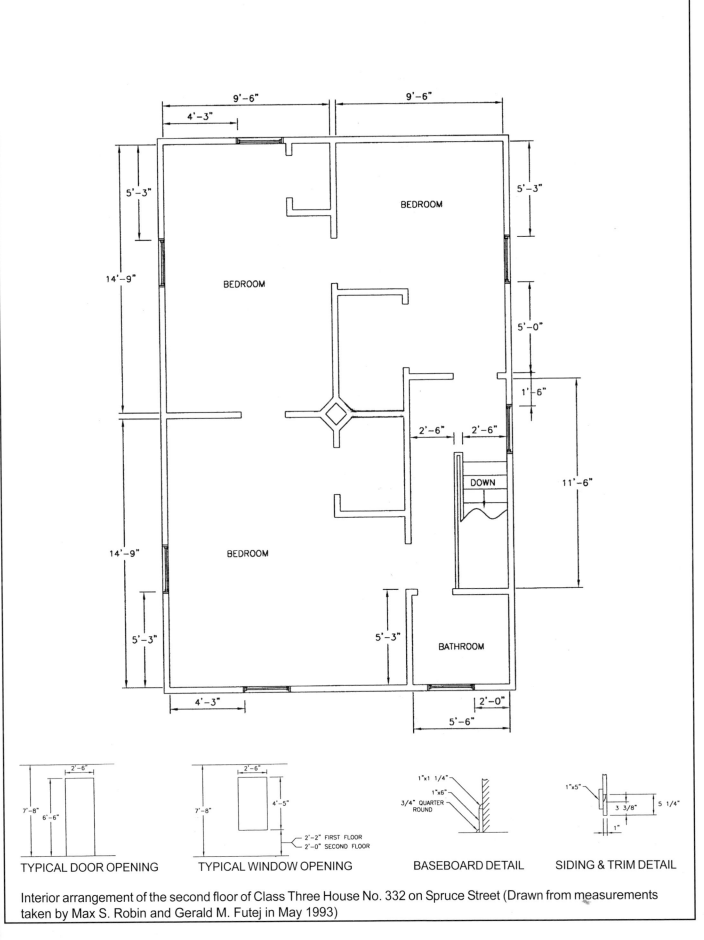

9'-6" 9'-6"

4'-3"

BEDROOM

5'-3" 5'-3"

14'-9"

BEDROOM

5'-0"

1'-6"

2'-6" 2'-6"

11'-6"

DOWN

14'-9"

BEDROOM

5'-3"

5'-3"

BATHROOM

4'-3" 2'-0"

5'-6"

2'-6"

7'-8"
6'-6"

TYPICAL DOOR OPENING

2'-6"

4'-5"

7'-8"

2'-2" FIRST FLOOR
2'-0" SECOND FLOOR

TYPICAL WINDOW OPENING

1"x1 1/4"

1"x6"

3/4" QUARTER
ROUND

BASEBOARD DETAIL

1"x5"

3 3/8"

5 1/4"

1"

SIDING & TRIM DETAIL

Interior arrangement of the second floor of Class Three House No. 332 on Spruce Street (Drawn from measurements taken by Max S. Robin and Gerald M. Futej in May 1993)

83

The Parlor and Dining Room of a typical Class Three House at Cass. (above) The ceiling register above the archway allows heat from the wood stove to rise to the second floor. Restored for tourist rental by the Cass Scenic Railroad State Park, access to the second floor is via the open staircase to the right of the Parlor. (below)

One of the three bedrooms on the second floor of a restored Class Three House. This one is at the top of the stairway.

Modernized kitchen with all the comforts of home awaits the next visitor. The hallway at center leads to the front door. The door to the left of the hallway leads to a storage area under the stairway. (All interior photos by Sonny Burruss)

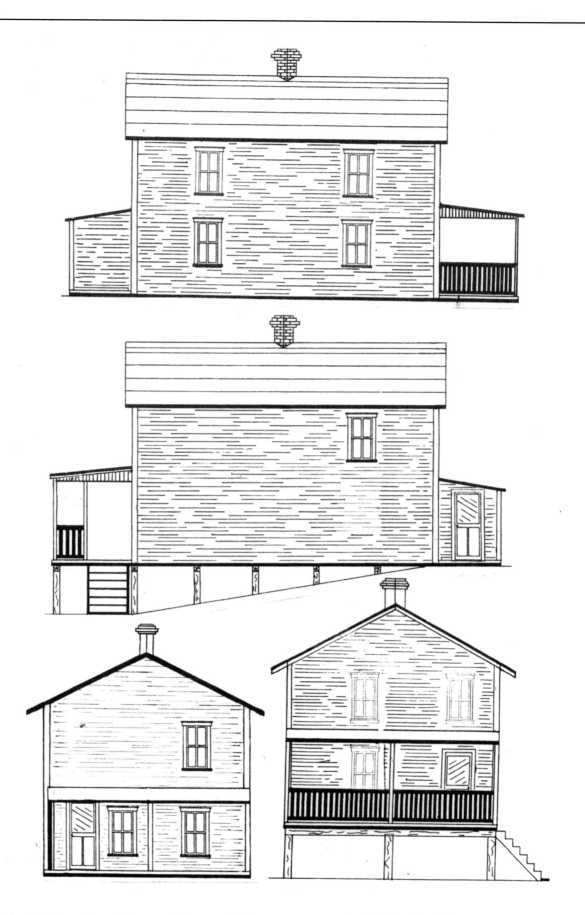

Drawings for the Class Three Houses at Cass made from measurements taken by Linda Tompkins-Mortinsen in 1978. These are included in an HO scale kit offered for sale by Keystone Locomotive Works of Pulteney, NY. (Courtesy of Keystone Locomotive Works, P.O. Box 206, Pulteney, NY, 14874)

First floor structure and concrete pier foundations used at Cass as seen during the dismantling of a house at "Slabtown" south of Cass. While not identical to the Class Three Houses used at Cass, these 20' by 30' frame houses shared a similar construction style. (Photographer unknown, collection of Richard Dale)

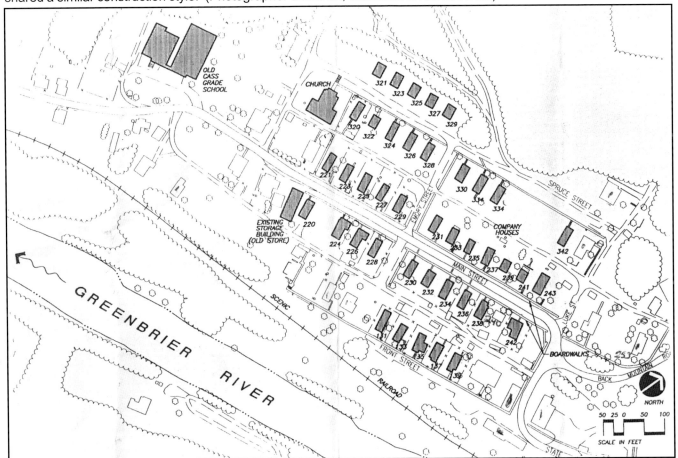

Map of Cass, WV and the residences owned by the Cass Scenic Railroad State Park. (Courtesy of Cass Scenic Railroad State Park)

Each house was provided with a fuel shed located along the alley behind the houses. This is the alley side of an old fuel shed at Cass. Coal was delivered through the doors by a chute from the coal truck. (Photo by Sonny Burruss)

The alley side of a rebuilt fuel shed with only one door, barely visible, near the left end. (Photo by Sonny Burruss)

The house side of a rebuilt fuel shed with entry doors for fuel removal or storage. (Photo by Sonny Burruss)

Class Two Houses No. 245 and No. 253 sit on a hill at the north end of Main Street. Both houses have front porches that wrap around the south side, with turned posts and railings significantly different than the Class Three Houses. Both of these houses are also one room deeper than the Class Threes. Note the circular vent window in the gable end. (Photographer unknown, Department of Highways Collection, West Virginia State Archives)

The Class Three Houses were originally built to a standardized floor plan. However, interior renovations and remodeling have sometimes resulted in specific houses and room dimensions varying from that floor plan. In spite of that, the houses still remain basically the same.

Class Two Houses, for use by office workers and division foremen, were of more varied designs and sizes, often situated on larger lots, corner lots, or sites away from other houses. The NRHP application describes them as: "Some of these are two-bays wide with a two-story side wing, which made them L-shaped, with three gabled ends. Others have three-bay facades, with a hip roof, center hall and stairway, and at least four windows on each side of the house. Houses No. 214 and No. 219 on Main Street are considered good examples of this construction style."

In some cases, Class Two Houses were built longer front to back. Virtually all of these houses have larger front porches and more detailed exterior decorations. Turned balusters and posts, fancy porch railings and a ventilator at the gable are typical on these houses. The NRHP application goes on to say "House No. 245, on an extension of Main Street, is typical of the Class Two dwellings. It sits high above Luke Street

on a sloping corner lot. When viewed from the north it is very like the better class-three houses, but exterior differences include a deeper porch on the front (east)

Rear of a Class Two House with L-shaped floor plan, two chimneys and round ventilator in the gable. (Photo by Sonny Burruss)

South and east sides of the Superintendent's House at the corner of Luke Street and Spruce, the only Company House at Cass with an outside chimney. (Photo by Sonny Burruss)

Front of the Superintendent's House from Luke Street. Reportedly used by Samuel Slaymaker, it was later used by J. Fred Weber and several of the State Park Superintendents. (Photo by Sonny Burruss)

South and east sides of the Doctor's House at Cass. Much larger than most of the other houses it is the only one with bay windows. (Photo by Sonny Burruss)

North side of the Doctor's House with its companion two story bay window. (Photo by Sonny Burruss)

The front (east side) of the Luke House. Built as a local residence for the owners of the West Virginia Pulp and Paper Company, it overlooks the Greenbrier River from high on the hill above Cass. (Photo by Sonny Burruss)

side which extended around a portion of the south side. The porch has turned posts with braces and attractive railings. Windows are double-hung sash, with single-pane glass. In the front gable is a round ventilator close under the eaves. At the rear is a one-story ell above a small basement, and a small porch is in the angle of the ell. A "German" siding was used on the house and its dependencies, and wood stairs and a board walk lead from Luke Street to the porch. The interior plan is like the class-three house except that the slightly larger size gives space for larger rooms. Other class two dwellings are at 131 and 139 Front Street, 219, 243, 251 and 253 Main and 344 Spruce."

The Class One Houses were intended for use by managers. They were generally larger than even the Class Two Houses. Grouped toward the north end of Cass, they were all two story houses, many with significant additions added over the years. The interiors reflected the more expensive construction of the time and the Company connection with the lumber industry. Wood panelled walls and specialty flooring designs contributed to the elegance of these houses.

The Superintendent's house, the Doctor's house, the four houses along Back Mountain Road and, of course, The Luke House (also known as "The Club House") all were in the Class One category.

The houses available for rent today have been completely renovated by the State. They offer full sleeping, bathing, and cooking facilities for as many as six or eight guests. Including those with full ADA accessibility for handicapped visitors.

A weekend in one of these houses is like stepping back in time and visiting grandma's. They're comfortable, cozy, and very warm with a nice fire burning in the parlor wood stove. Just remember to bring your own kindling! Oh yes, make a reservation in advance. They go quickly on special event weekends.

The three story high north side of the Luke House provides a feel for just how large it is. Also known as "The Club House" it provided space to accommodate visitors for both business and social occasions. (Photo by Sonny Burruss)

The rear (west side) of the Luke House. Used as a permanent residence by Emory P. Schaefer and his family. Do you think it was large enough for five girls? (Photo by Sonny Burruss)

TO THE NEW OCCUPANTS

This house has been our home since September 15, 1942. We have been told that it was built about 1916, but it is well built of good materials, and should last a century. The panneling in the living room is native white pine, with spruce ceiling, installed in 1947. It has birch panneling in the halls, with spruce ceiling installe in 1948. You will find that the fireplace really works, and should give you many happy hours.

We hope that you like birds, as they will be looking for food because we have supplied them for 18 years. Watch for the evening Grossbecks about November 15th. They like sunflower seeds as do the Cardinals. You will enjoy watching the ground squirrels as they store acorns for the winter. Of course to have birds and squirrels, it will be neccesary to keep the cats away. Listen for the quail in the pasture.

Our daughter Jennie had a black dachshund " an only pet" received as a Christmas present in 1947 and named "Jingle Bells" which became "jingle." Jingle was a faithful guardian of our properties, and to our sorrow, was found dead in her bed, on January 1, 1960. You will find her grave. under the old apple tree, in the northwest corner of the yard. Wewould appreciate it if you would respect Jingle's resting place.

The trees have grown taller, since our arrival. The white pine at the kitchen window was about 12" tall 18 years ago. For many years we have been putting lights on it at Christmas.

We hope that you will be happy in the house, which has been our home these many years, and will continue to improve both the house and the grounds.

J. Fred Weber, Jr.
Lucy G. Weber
Jennie Weber
Susie Weber

This letter from Fred Weber was found on the mantle of the Superintendent's house at Cass. It was found by Richard Dale when his family moved into the house. Mr. Dale was Superintendent of the Cass Scenic Railroad State Park 1977-1986. Mr. Weber was the Mower Lumber Company Superintendent at Cass 1942-1960. (courtesy Richard Dale)

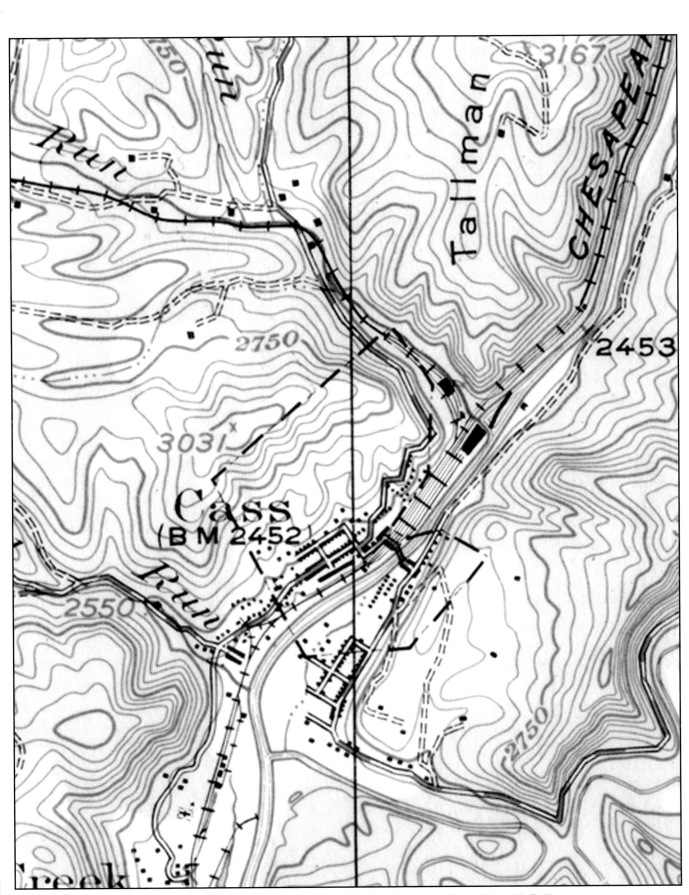

1922 Geological Survey map of Cass. (U.S. Department of the Interior, collection of Don McFall)

John and Christine Glaab's house at Cass was built in 1906. It's restoration started in 1987 and is nearly complete. It too is 100 years and still counting. (Photo by John Glaab)

Restoring a House at Cass

by John Glaab

For over 20 years my wife and I have been in love with the mountain country around Cass. We would go camping, ride the Cass Scenic Railroad, and generally do the "touristy" type things one does in that area. At Christine's suggestion, we began looking for property in the area on which to build a house. We talked to real estate people and subscribed to the local weekly paper, *The Pocahontas Times*. We read the real estate ads, looked at land and found some things we liked, but never well enough to commit.

In the spring of 1987, Christine found an ad in the *Times* for an upcoming house auction in Cass. So with no real plan in mind, we attended just to get an idea of what was available. People began arriving about 8:30 a.m. and started looking over the house. This was not a really big crowd, maybe 25-30 people; lots of lookers, but few people really interested in buying.

Although most of the town is now owned by the State, some of the houses are privately owned. When Mower Lumber Company, and earlier West

Virginia Pulp and Paper Company, owned the town, a resident could buy a house from the Company with the provision that it would only be sold back to the Company and at the original selling price plus the value of any improvements. When the State purchased the town in 1976, the few houses with ownership under this system were given clear titles. In the case of this house, Roger Mower was the owner, he used it as his vacation residence for several years. Title was not transferred when the State purchased the town, and the property subsequently was sold to another private owner.

We located the house situated on the hill directly behind the depot on a row with three other houses. These (and a fourth house now long gone) had been the residences of administrators and managers for the lumber operations. One was used by the mill manager, one by the rail operations manager, and one by the manager of the commissary. The one being auctioned was used by the comptroller during the 1920's and 30's. The locals called the area "Big Bug Hill" because the middle managers or "big bugs" lived there.

The location on Back Mountain Road gave it good proximity to the railroad (a huge plus!). It had city water and sewage and appeared to be habitable. Inspection showed us a large house, originally built in 1906, in the general configuration of all the Cass Company houses with living room, dining room, and kitchen downstairs and two or three bedrooms upstairs. It was added onto at least twice, so that it had five bedrooms and two baths on the second floor and seven rooms on the first. One upper bedroom and a lower parlor had the look of an addition for servant's quarters. Generally speaking, a pretty fancy house for Cass!

The place needed help. The servants' wing had sunk about eight inches and the sills were rotted. The foundation of this part was concrete piers, which were unstable. The slope of the land caused water to collect at the foundation, and this was the cause of the problem. The exterior had not been maintained in years; white paint was flaking everywhere and the roof leaked. There were three porches, all in sad shape with rotted boards, missing steps and some really ratty lattice work.

Inside things weren't so bad. The main part of the house was square and sound. All the windows were intact. Not much cracked plaster, but every room was wallpapered, walls and ceilings! The floors were all oak and maple hardwood, but needed some repair and sanding. The woodwork was a strong point, all chestnut and in excellent shape. A large, elegant stairway, sound and beautifully finished, rose from the foyer to a landing, and then continued up to the second floor. Since these houses were built when the railroad and mill were most important and the road was a minor convenience, the foyer is in what many would now consider the "back" of the house, away from the road.

The kitchen was dated with electric stove, double sink, and inexpensive cabinets. Off the kitchen was an 8 foot by 15 foot butler's pantry in really rough shape with exposed piping, holes in the floor patched with tin can lids, and plaster falling from the walls and ceiling.

Outside was a small garage, badly in need of paint. Steps and walkways were in really poor shape. Too many trees kept the house from ever getting any sun. What remained of the former landscaping had returned to nature.

So we bought the house and began the restoration. Our idea was to restore the house to what it might have looked like in the 1920-1930 era. The heyday of the lumbering era at Cass.

I think it's fair to say that Christine and I had no idea what we had gotten into. A careful inspection showed that the part of the house thought to be the servants quarters had severe water damage to its foundation. It needed to be jacked up, new continuous foundations poured and new sills and flooring installed. This highlighted that we had a severe surface water problem and we needed to install a network of French drains and retaining walls around the Back Mountain Road side of the house.

The porches were in worse shape. Years of neglect and a variety of wood boring insects had taken their toll. Wood boring beetles, carpenter ants, and bees had all taken a turn. There was some good news, no termites. The sills and flooring were replaced, the porches leveled and new railings installed.

While all of this was going on, Christine and her mother were removing all of the wallpaper, layers and layers of wallpaper. This went on for months. I patched and repaired all the plaster. Many walls had been papered directly over the brown coat plaster. There was no finish coat. Well, care to guess who got to skim coat all the walls? We decided not to strip the wallpaper from the ceilings, but to drywall over them. It turned out great. Then Christine painted and painted and painted.

Then came the big project of repainting the house exterior. I hired a crew of local laborers for this. For almost three months, four to six people worked five to six days a week removing old paint and repainting. The exterior is German siding, so they used heat guns and hand scrapers, then belt sanded.

The entire house was scraped down to bare wood and primed. While we were scraping off the old paint we found some very good samples of the apparently original three tone grey-green colors, which I recognized as C&O station colors of the era. I started checking on the dates for the construction of the house and the station. They were built the same year! I can only imagine how the house came to be painted the same color as the station.

We set out to match the colors and paint the house as it was originally. This did not go over well with all of the parties interested in Cass preservations.

Some felt that the house should be left white on the assumption that all the houses were always white. But with the help of some local old-timers who let others know that all Cass houses weren't always white, and the evidence of the original boards with the green color, we charged ahead. We now have a three-tone gray-green house with lighter walls, medium trim and darker porches.

With the house painted, and the porches and general structure intact, I began to tackle the mechanical systems. All new plumbing, new electrical wiring and a new heating system were installed. We kept the original radiators and piping and installed a new hot water boiler. There had been a little hallway from the kitchen to the front foyer. We had been told that this was to allow the servants to answer the front door without intruding on the people who might be in the sitting room. This got converted into a half bath. Christine and I figured it would be a long time before we needed a servant's hallway (never). The hardwood floors got sanded and the upstairs bathrooms redone with period fixtures. The floor in the dining area had been severely damaged over the years and I took the opportunity to replace it. I made the flooring and installed a patterned floor in what is referred to as the "log-cabin" design. It's a term borrowed from quilting and describes a style reminiscent of a picture frame surround by a series of picture frames. The floor is made of red oak, cherry and black walnut. It came out rather nicely.

Light fixtures were next. Almost all the rooms had some type of center-mounted ceiling fixture. These were removed, polished, rewired and reinstalled. Several antique fixtures of the same (brass mission) style were purchased to replace broken or missing units.

Christine's kitchen was the break from restoration to upscale remodeling. A three deep sink, butcher's block, six burner-two oven gas range with matching hood, and matching upright freezer and refrigerator form the basis. I'm still working on the cabinets.

The north side of the Glaab House with entrances to the kitchen, at right, and the servant's quarters, at left. (Photo by John Glaab)

The house has been furnished largely with period furniture purchased at country auctions. During the late 1980's and early 1990's a lot of farms were sold in the area and there was an estate auction just about every weekend. Antique furniture from the 1920's and 1930's was plentiful and reasonably priced. By the mid 1990's the antique dealers from just about everywhere in the mid-Atlantic Region had discovered the area, and prices went up sharply!

Although we wanted to stay as true to the original appearance and materials as possible, we did use some high tech materials that have better weather resistance. Our gutters look like half round metal, but are plastic reproductions. Our exterior trim boards are PVC not wood. Our roofing, although it looks like the original roll roofing of the period, is actually a rubberized membrane.

The north side porch looking east toward the Greenbrier River. (Photo by John Glaab)

It's been 20 years since we bought the house and we aren't done yet. Both Christine and I enjoy restoring the house.

It's hard to say what would have happened to this house if we hadn't purchased it. The State has a history of buying up properties like this one, to consolidate their holding in the park area. However, the park system suffers from a shortage of funding, and is often barely able to stabilize the buildings, let alone restore them. I'd like to believe that we have saved this house for generations to come, and that future visitors to Cass will have the ability to see what one of the manager's houses looked like in its prime. I only wish it were possible for more Cass houses to be obtained by private individuals willing to expend the effort to restore them.

The road to house restoration may be challenging, but the end result can be very satisfying. If you have a chance walk by our house and say hello!

The restored "front" porch faces the Greenbrier River. A quiet place to listen to the whisper of the wind in the trees, the rush of the water around the rocks, and the melodious whistles of the locomotives on the Cass Scenic Railroad. (Photo by John Glaab)

Prototype of an HO scale model of the Doctor's House at Cass. (Photo by John Glaab)

Doctor's House in HO Scale
by John Glaab

Over time Cass becomes not just a place but a state of mind. Since buying and restoring a house there, it's hard to separate Cass from the rest of life. A great deal of effort has been expended to restore many of the residences at Cass. The restoration process, however, often lags behind the natural process of structural deterioration. Many of the Class Three Houses at Cass have been lost and several more may have terminal deterioration. The available State funds can only go so far.

In an effort to maintain the memory of some of the larger structures at Cass I took up the challenge of

developing an HO scale kit of the Doctor's House. A formidable and unique structure at Cass, this house may also succumb to nature. However, it is possible to own your own copy, albeit in 1:87 scale. The kits, priced at $90.00, are available from Peach Creek Shops, call 301-498-9071.